THE YUGOSLAV TRAGEDY

By the same author

After Imperialism (1963)

What Economics is About (1970)

Essays on Imperialism (1972)

From Labourism to Socialism (1972)

The Economics of Imperialism (1974)

Information at Work (1978)

Models in Political Economy (1984, revised 1995)

European Union: Fortress or Democracy? (1991)

Short Changed: Africa and World Trade
(with Pauline Tiffen, 1992)

Fair Trade: Reform and Realities in the International Trading System (1993)

A European Recovery Programme: Restoring Full Employment
(edited with Ken Coates, 1993)

Africa's Choices: After Thirty Years of the World Bank (1995)

*Democracy versus Capitalism:
With Some Old Questions for New Labour*
(with Hugo Radice, 1995)

SOCIALIST RENEWAL

The Yugoslav Tragedy

Lessons for Socialists

MICHAEL BARRATT BROWN

Spokesman
for
European Labour Forum

First published in Great Britain in 1996 by
Spokesman
Bertrand Russell House
Gamble Street
Nottingham, England
Tel. 0115 9708318
Fax. 0115 9420433

Publications list available on request

British Library Cataloguing in Publication Data available on request from the British Library.

ISBN 0-85124-590-0 cloth
ISBN 0-85124-588-9 paper

Printed by the Russell Press Ltd, Nottingham
(Tel. 0115 9784505)

Contents

Map		vi
I.	Introduction: The Nation-State	1
II.	The Question of a Third Balkan War	21
III.	Socialism and Nationalism	43
IV.	Conclusion: The Lessons	73

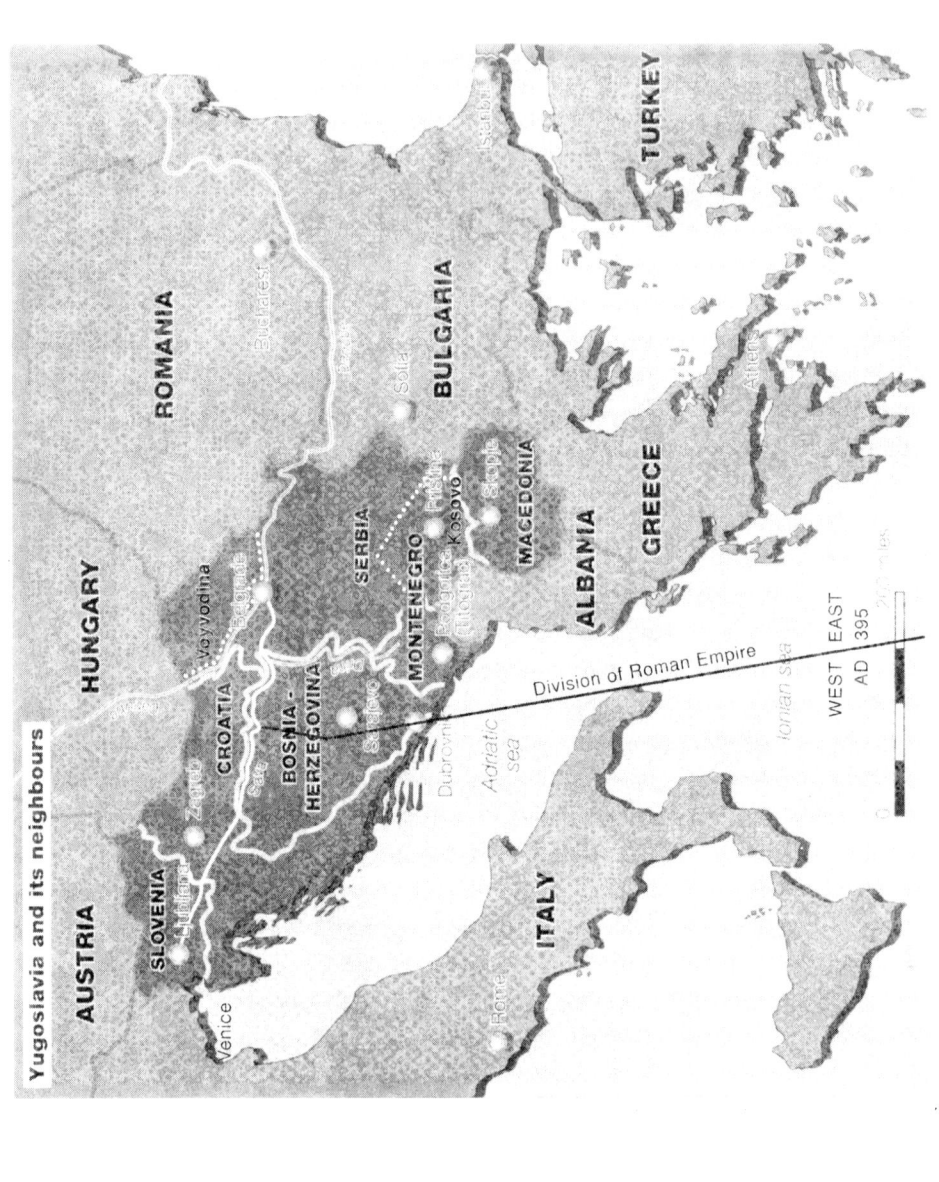

Yugoslavia and its neighbours

AUSTRIA

SLOVENIA
Ljubljana
Venice

HUNGARY

CROATIA
Zagreb

Vojvodina

Belgrade

BOSNIA - HERZEGOVINA
Sarajevo

SERBIA

MONTENEGRO
Podgorica

Kosovo
Priština

ROMANIA
Bucharest

BULGARIA
Sofia

MACEDONIA
Skopje

ALBANIA

GREECE

TURKEY
Istanbul

Athens

Adriatic sea

Dubrovnik

ITALY
Rome

Ionian Sea

Division of Roman Empire

WEST   EAST
AD 395

I
The Nation-State

An important aspect of socialist renewal is the need to expose and to challenge myths about socialism. I am not the one to do this work in relation to the claims to socialism of the Soviet Union or of China or of most of the Eastern Europe regimes before 1989. Others with far more knowledge and experience can do that. I have, however, some knowledge and close experience of the meaning and practice of the particular form of socialism which developed in Yugoslavia. This was rightly seen as showing a somewhat different model from either that of the Soviet Union and its satellites or that of China. The Yugoslav model disintegrated at almost the same time as the Soviet and East European and has thus tended to be written off as the same only worse, or alternatively just a preview of what we may see developing more widely throughout what was once the Soviet Union.

All the socialist experiments have to be seen in the historical context of the countries where they took place. This would be obvious enough just from considering the great differences in the history of China or that of Russia and the peoples which formed the Soviet Union. It may be particularly necessary in considering the Yugoslav case. Since all these experiments were undertaken by men and women who believed that Marx had supplied the key to understanding the necessary conditions for social change, it has been assumed that they can all be lumped together and called 'the socialist failure'. This came naturally to those who saw the world after 1917 as being divided into two camps — capitalist and socialist — which ended with the defeat of one by the other.

To the extent that two camps actually existed, the camps were formed of nation-states divided by national interests and not by class interest. Most of the fighting, including two world wars, took place between rival powers inside one or other of the camps, in fact mainly inside the capitalist camp. Those who have seen the Third World as a part of the socialist camp have argued that the most recent wars like the Viet Nam war, the battle for the Falkland Islands or the Gulf War could be comprehended within a two camp framework. While this might just be claimed for the Viet Nam war, Soviet support for the Viet Cong was minimal and the Chinese actually attacked them. Neither General Galtieri nor Saddam Hussein ever claimed to be socialists, and in neither case did the Soviet Union or Russia come to their defence.

A world of nation-states

The point that I am wanting to make is that we live in a world of nation-states in which the appeal of nationalism has been sedulously propagated by the state builders who have been busy creating their own states out of the several nations for the last two centuries. This has been just as much the case with those who were guided by Marx as those who saw themselves as followers of Adam Smith. The whole socialist experiment has been conducted within the framework of the nation-state. That was the lesson learnt from Lenin, who, whatever he had once believed about the freedom of peoples, created a Soviet state out of a dozen or more nations. Stalin put the seal on this compact which only came unstuck in 1989.

The nation-state was in most cases a Nineteenth Century creation, designed to provide a framework for the development of capitalism. For this purpose, that is to provide a viable market size and critical mass of capital accumulation, a state had often to be larger than the population and territory of any single nation. The United Kingdom of the English, Scottish, Welsh and Irish was the first. Most others were created after the American and French revolutions. Thus, Yugoslavia served the same purpose as the United Kingdom, although its formation took place more than two centuries later. How far the nation-state became crucial to the development of capitalism can be seen from its combination of economic and political roles.

In Nineteenth Century Britain, despite all the talk of *laissez-faire* and a 'nightwatchman state', British capitalism could not have developed without the breaking down of local tolls and markets, agrarian society and common lands and their replacement by a new framework of life. The Enclosure Acts, a Royal Mail, a Bank of England, Company Laws, Police Forces, state education and sanitary legislation, central and local government services and above all an army and navy to maintain colonial rule over half the globe were all needed to protect and extend the capitalist system long before the provisions of the welfare state became a further necessity.

To override existing local, community and cultural loyalties of the peoples who had sometimes called themselves 'nations', a new nationalism had to be created for the state. The word 'nation' had to serve both for its old meaning of 'peoples' or 'tribes', literally 'breeds' and its new sense of statehood. The state builders of the Nineteenth Century had to create new nations and did so with all the symbolism of a national flag, national weights and measures including a national coinage, national days of celebration and remembrance, national monuments and all the power and glory of national armed forces and often of a royal household.

The origins of nationalism

Elie Kedourie in what is perhaps the best known book on 'nationalism', opens his work with the following words:

'Nationalism is a doctrine invented in Europe at the beginning of the Nineteenth Century. It pretends to supply a criterion for the determination of the unit of population proper to enjoy a government exclusively its own, for the legitimate exercise of power in the state, and for the right organisation of a society of states. Briefly, the doctrine holds that humanity is naturally divided into nations, that nations are known by certain characteristics which can be ascertained, and that the only legitimate type of government is national self-government.'

This was the challenge of the French Revolution to the rule of absolute monarchs, by which the claim was made that sovereignty no longer rested in an individual hereditary sovereign but in the nation. 'The Declaration of the Rights of Man and of the Citizen', prefixed to the French constitution of 1791, proclaimed that

'The principle of sovereignty resides essentially in the Nation; no body of men, no individual, can exercise authority that does not emanate expressly from it.'

Up until that time the idea of 'nations' in France as elsewhere referred simply to people coming from different regions, with different languages or dialects. From then on it referred to those 'living under one common law and represented by the same legislature.' Kedourie seeks to demonstrate the philosophical underpinnings of the sovereignty of nations in the claim of Immanuel Kant for individual self-determination as the supreme good, and so it must be with national self-determination. Even more important was the critique by Jean-Jacques Rousseau of a social contract between ruler and ruled, which had been explored earlier by John Locke in defending the English revolution of 1688. The issue was and still is the relationship between the individual, his or her community and the state. The power of the state had in the past been extended for the self aggrandisement of the rulers and justified by the protection offered to the ruled, whether as individuals or communities. But nascent capitalism demanded a different kind of state with a different source of legitimation.

The difference lay in the fact that, whereas the absolute monarch or feudal prince derived his wealth by force from individual impost or servile labour or else from collective tribute (literally 'divided among the tribes'), the capitalist derived his from free labour and the nation-state from taxation, consented to by those holding property and thereby qualifying for the franchise. Freedom from authoritarian rule was a great and glorious event. The welcome given by poets and pamphleteers to the American and French revolutions bears witness to this fact. The representation of the people in the nation-states that were created proved more difficult to ensure, even as more and more of the people, who had no property qualification, were added to the electorate. Having no property, they were not 'stakeholders' but still had to be incorporated in the state because of their sheer numbers. At the base of society patriarchal slavery had been replaced by wage slavery, what Marx called the 'veiled slavery of the wage workers in Europe', although for long, as he averred, this 'needed for its pedestal slavery pure and simple in the new world'. How were these masses to be made to feel part of the nation?

Since the new nation-states of the Nineteenth Century were being created out of diverse peoples and communities, and what was being required of them was free labour and voluntary consent to authority, the individual citizen (in the UK he or she remained a 'subject') had to become increasingly identified with the new nation and nation-state. In his *Addresses to the German Nation* in 1808 the first German nationalist, Johann Gottlieb Fichte, asked not only for a state that maintained internal peace but one that created man's freedom both materially and also spiritually. By merging their will in the state, Fichte asserted that individuals find their freedom. In the excitement of bringing down the rule of all the petty princelings of Central Europe, which were choking the peoples' initiative, such rhetoric won many hearts and minds. As the reality of wage slavery emerged for most, some more positive acts of cohesion were required than mere verbal apostrophe. Social liberation had to follow national liberation and the nation-state had ultimately to become the guardian of cohesion in a political economy that tended by its very nature to polarise wealth and poverty.

National liberation

The first generation of nation-states emerged in Western Europe. They represented a liberation from the absolute and feudal authority of hereditary rulers. A second generation in Eastern Europe and a third in the European empires spread across Asia and Africa represented a liberation from imperial rulers. To be precise, the United States and the South American nation-states liberated themselves from Spanish and British rule at much the same time as the first European nation-states were being created. The struggles to liberate themselves from foreign empires were seen as national liberation movements. They aroused the same excitement and enthusiasm, particularly among the young, as had the earlier generation of struggles against absolute power and feudal rule.

Indeed, since imperial power was wielded by rulers who came from distant lands and often had different coloured skins and sought always to impose their own customs and language upon the peoples they conquered, the anticipation of freedom was much the greater and its achievement the more intoxicating. The idea of Yugoslav liberation from the Austro-Hungarian empire fired a whole generation of Serbian, Croatian, Macedonian and Slovene young nationalists and it was one of them whose murder of the heir to the Austrian Empire in Sarajevo set alight the flames of the 1914-18 war. The hopes and fears of these young people are marvellously recreated by

THE NATION-STATE

Bosnia's greatest writer Ivo Andric' at the end of his novel *The Bridge over the Drina*.

Toma Galus is a Serb and his friend Fehim Bahtijarevic a Moslem. Both are students at the University of Sarajevo. They are seated on the parapet of the bridge over the Drina at Višegrad, which once marked both the frontier and the crossing point between the East and the West — between the Ottoman and the Austro-Hungarian empires. Galus is proclaiming the destiny of 'young and free nations, appearing for the first time on the stage of history, to express themselves directly':

'Modern nationalism will triumph over religious diversities and outmoded prejudice, will liberate our people from foreign influence and exploitation. Then will the national state be born.' and he goes on to describe

'all the advantages and beauties of the new national state which was to rally all the Southern Slavs around Serbia as a sort of Piedmont [the rallying centre of Italian unification] on the basis of complete national unity, religious tolerance and civil equality. His speech mixed up bold words of uncertain meaning and expression that accurately expressed the needs of modern life, the deepest desires of a race, most of which were to remain only desires, and the justified and attainable demands of everyday reality. It mingled the great truths which had ripened through the generations but which only youth could perceive in advance and dare to express, with the eternal illusions which are never extinguished but never attain realisation, for one generation of youth hands them on to the next like that mythological torch.'

His friend Bahtijarevic remains silent, even when Galus goes on to describe what the new state will accomplish — in fermenting new ideas, encouraging new deeds, putting up great buildings, 'building new, greater and better bridges, not to link foreign centres with conquered lands, but to link our own lands with the rest of the world.'

THE YUGOSLAV TRAGEDY

Social liberation

As so often before, once again the achievement of a nation-state, even one large enough to be economically viable for capitalist development, left most of the Yugoslav peoples in 1919 no better off and, in many cases, with the same foreign companies exploiting them on the lands and in the mines and factories as before. The same had for long been the experience of the South American peoples in their nation-states created out of the Spanish and Portuguese empires in the Nineteenth Century. The same was to be the experience of the peoples of those nation-states created in the 1950s from the colonial territories of the European powers. This process was given the designation of neo-colonialism, the difference being that the nationalist leaders, while taking over the political powers which the Europeans had relinquished, had agreed to co-operate in the economic exploitation of their own peoples.

The concept of national liberation struggles against colonial rule caused much trouble for Marxists who had always regarded the appeal to a common national identity as an attempt to displace a common class solidarity. As a result, some Marxists felt bound to call national liberation struggles 'class struggles' and when independence from colonial rule was achieved, this was naturally welcomed. But in many quarters it was welcomed quite uncritically without questions being asked either about the social liberation of the people or about the mix of peoples generally quite arbitrarily merged together. For these new nation-states were created on the very territories which colonial rulers had carved out for their own purposes. In Africa, for example, over 50 nation-states were formed, some of them comprising no more than a million people, some tens of millions, while many crossed the boundaries of historic tribes and communities. Attempts to establish cohesion through nation building have been unsuccessful. At the same time, every

8

approach to promoting regional organisations has been disrupted from outside.

What is appropriately called the 'balkanisation' of Africa has provided the opportunity for outside economic and financial powers to continue to divide and conquer and render nugatory all African efforts to construct together their own African road to development. The result has been that, far from uniting together against a common enemy, communities of ethnic and historical nations have torn each other apart in competing for external favours and for the declining value in world markets of Africa's available resources.

Basil Davidson writing on 'the challenge of nationalism' as he saw it both in his war-time and subsequent experience of the struggle for Yugoslavia, and in his long involvement in the struggles of African peoples, has summed up the problem in the following way in his *The Black Man's Burden: The Curse of the Nation-State.*

'The jubilant crowds celebrating [African] independence were not inspired by a "national consciousness" that "demanded the nation," any more than were the peasants and their coevals in the nation-states crystallised some decades earlier from Europe's old internal empires. They were inspired by the hope of more and better food and shelter.' And he goes on

'As long as the "social" held its lead over the "national", this continued to be so. But it did not continue to hold that lead for long. Once the national sovereignties were declared, the arena was fixed for rivalry over the resources within that arena; and the rivalry was bound to become abrasive and therefore divisive, if only because the resources were in short supply. This divisive rivalry was then discovered to be "tribalism": that is, the reinforcement of kinship and other local scale alliances competing against other such alliances.'

The warning for the 'balkanised' states of the former Soviet Union and for ex-Yugoslavia is an obvious one, and it is rendered the more serious by the challenge to the historic role of the nation-state in the current process of the globalisation of capital.

A future for the nation-state?

If the old nation-state is under challenge from below, by fissiparous movements into smaller nationalisms, it is equally under pressure from above. The European nation-states were supposed to be large enough in markets and capital accumulation to be viable economic as well as political units. The founding fathers of the United States had given warning that, in a summary of the views of one of them, James Madison in his appropriately named *Federalist Papers* of 1788 (as quoted in Kedourie's *Nationalism*):

> 'only . . . a sovereign government of truly continental scope, can assure a non-oppressive popular rule. A republican leviathan is necessary to secure life, liberty and property from the tyranny of local majorities. The extended republic is not simply a means of adapting popular rule to new political realities, but an inherently desirable corrective for deep intrinsic defects in the politics of the small popular regime'.

(The reference to 'leviathan' is to a biblical sea monster with which Thomas Hobbes in 1651, two years after the execution of a King of England, compared the autocratic state. He believed that it had both to be 'raised up' and 'drawn out on the hook', in Job's language — that is both set over the people as a protection against their own worst instincts and yet kept under control.)

Small states have not only shown the intrinsic defects of oppressive popular rule of which Madison warned; they have recently been rendered incapable of playing the role in the development of capitalism for which they were first conceived. There has been much argument in recent years about the viability of the nation-state — just as more and more are added to their number. Their role of providing a political and economic framework for the free exchange of goods and factors of production combined with economic growth in a competitive world market is under challenge.

That longed-for national sovereignty in economic matters has been reduced to nothing by the growth in the size and multinational operations of the modern corporation. Only the very largest and most powerful states can today manage their own moneys and control the disequilibrating tendencies of private capital accumulation. These giant companies treat the smaller states as supplicants bidding for resources with offers of cheap labour, and softer standards on pollution or health and safety. There is still a role for the nation-state in a capitalist system, but it is no longer a sovereign role.

What then is the prospect? Can the great business corporations that dominate the world economy themselves agree to merge their interests, as Karl Kautsky once dreamed it might be before the First World War? Is this the role of the IMF and the World Bank to provide a common framework for their capital accumulation? The question for the corporations will then be how to manage not only the markets but the competition between them in the production and commercialisation processes since each is driven to accumulate at the expense of the others. As the limits of their co-operation lie within the framework of great power agreement, achieving such an agreement lies beyond them. John Maynard Keynes could only propose it at Bretton Woods at the end of a most destructive war, with the fear of the Soviet Union beckoning to the peoples of the world to follow an alternative way if the great powers did not agree.

It seems, then, that the major nation-states will have to find ways of working together at levels below the global — rather to maintain their power than to reduce their power. This is the theme of Alan Milward's two extended studies *The European Rescue of the Nation-State* and *The Frontier of National Sovereignty: History and Theory, 1945-1992* (both published by Routledge in 1994). They have been the subject of a massive two piece inquiry by Perry Anderson in the *London Review of Books* on 'The Europe to Come' (January 4th and 25th, 1996). Reduced to its simplest terms, Milward's thesis is that 'the strength of the European Community lies after all in the weakness of the nation-state'. The smaller states need the protection both political and economic of a larger union with a federal constitution. The two largest states — Germany and France — need mutual protection against the danger of drifting into another life or death battle of a Great War, but neither their people nor those of the United Kingdom, Italy or Spain are ready to dissolve what they believe to be their sovereignty in a United States of Europe.

The problem for European statesmen is to find a source of cohesion among 12 or 15 or 20 or more nations all with their own languages and traditions. The Seventeenth Century philosophers sought for consent from the people for a nation-state that would in effect supplant the diverse languages and customs of the several peoples brought together within it. The United States assimilated into one English speaking union the many peoples that settled in its territory, having first destroyed the Indian people and enslaved those of African origin. The most recent wave of immigrants — from south of the Rio Grande and from Puerto Rico — have hardly yet been assimilated. They have retained their Spanish language. Often illegal immigrants, they are excluded from the body politic and along with millions of others, whites as well as blacks, take no part in political life, the largest proportion of US citizens casting votes in Presidential elections never exceeding 50%.

Side by side with the false consciousness of national identity, there has always remained in most individuals a sense of community origins and of kinship associations. These do not entirely die way, but re-emerge in moments of national or individual crisis. Loss of markets or of currency value and international standing, like the loss of a close relative, loss of job, loss of home and belongings drive most of those who suffer such losses back into the reassurance and support of what they think of as 'their own people.' It is one of the tragedies of modern life that in an advanced industrialised country like Britain the extended working class community of relatives and neighbours is almost extinct. What has taken its place for some is the club or the union at work, for others the sport or professional association, for others still the fellowship of common cultural interests, even occasionally of political interest and international concern.

It is for many a frightening fact that in the most popular of international sports — the competition to win the several football cups — fanatical enthusiasm can lead to crowd violence and even deaths. It is not without its lessons that the leaders and members of some of the most savage paramilitary groups in Bosnia were drawn from the fans of the rival football teams and that the first serious fighting between Serbs and Croats took place between fans at the end of a football match in Zagreb. And yet, the proliferation of international gatherings and conferences on every subject under the sun, the interest in discovering about the lives of other peoples, the passion for what are called 'ethnic' products, all go to show that there is another side to the human spirit, even today. It is this rich diversity that distinguishes human beings, which the nation-state could not eradicate, and that has suggested to Alan Milward that we may give our consent to local government, our allegiance to unions of states, and I would add, our interest to a wider world, and our love to 'our own people'.

The power of global capital

Today, it is said that the day of the nation-state is over. Certainly its capacity to give some expression to the aspirations of peoples has been challenged by the increasing globalisation of capital in giant companies operating transnationally. Instead of the nation-state providing a democratic forum in which the voices of the people could be heard, and the national economy managed with some concern for the people, it has become an instrument for global capital to manipulate. International institutions which were designed to assist the unity and advancement of peoples — the United Nations itself, the International Monetary Fund (IMF) and World Bank, the Food and Agricultural Organisation (FAO), the UN Conference on Trade and Development (UNCTAD), the UN Educational, Cultural and Scientific Organisation (UNESCO) — have been perverted to serve the interests of global capital, or had their funding withdrawn.

While two or three very large states — the USA, China, Japan, Germany, Russia perhaps — have enough economic power to enable their statesmen to make independent political decisions, those in the great number of medium-sized and small states — even ex-imperial Britain — must follow their leader. Their much-prized sovereignty dissolves the moment that the central banks of the USA, Japan or Germany alter their interest rates or one of the giant transnational companies threatens to withdraw its investment. But, while capital moves globally, the people are still held within the shell of the nation-state. Inter-national communication is not only discouraged by nationalist propaganda, but it is both difficult and expensive to organise. The *internet* opens up new channels, but for communication between individuals. Using the new technology for mass communication requires access to very big capital and is therefore concentrated in a very few hands, which naturally belong to those who will wish to preserve the power of capital. Nations which could once boast of having statesmen have now to make do with travelling salesmen for the private banks, the oil companies and the arms manufacturers.

The case of Yugoslavia should, however, give the owners and managers of transnational capital some cause for concern. An economy in collapse, with its workforce dismembered, whole populations impoverished, agriculture neglected, transport and communications disrupted, does not offer either a market or a supply of labour which can be incorporated as a source of strength into the global system. It is one thing to sell surplus guns and distribute surplus food in one or two areas of the world. It is quite another to reduce a whole region to ruins. It may indeed be possible to marginalise whole continents like Africa, where foreign capital investment has been reduced almost to zero by the breakdown under World Bank debt management of even the most basic infrastructural state support that such investment depends on. Such marginalisation, however, cannot be too widely extended or there will remain nothing to exploit and no one to sell to. A labour force desperate for work at any price can, of course, be set to work in any number of *maquiladoras* (enterprise zone sweatshops) but it will not be able to afford the goods that it produces. Even the lean production of post-Fordist industry needs markets. If the nation-state is a dead-end for the people; it can become a booby-trap for capital.

Democratic power established by working class struggles within the nation-state seemed to have won bigger concessions from capital than internationalism was ever able to do. But, the nation-states are now being divided and conquered by capital, as groups of workers once were. In the meantime some of the workers in the more advanced capitalist countries have had a taste of a better life. As unemployment in face of new technological advances now threatens even those with highly sought after traditional skills, they have two alternatives: they can continue to seek the protection of the nation-state, even of a European fortress of nation-states; or they can support the struggles for better wages and conditions for the whole of global labour. Small and medium sized countries and vulnerable groups of workers will easily fall prey to the blandishments of the nationalists, with their high sounding offers of national protection. It may do them no good. This is perhaps the most telling lesson for socialists that Yugoslavia has to offer.

THE YUGOSLAV TRAGEDY

None of this, of course, is so new. The actions of national leaders were never so altruistically concerned with their peoples' needs as they were presented for public consumption. The defence of 'our national interests' — at Suez, on the Falkland Islands, in the Gulf or in all the wars of empire — was always one thing for the colonial investors, the oil companies and armament firms, quite another for the soldiers, sailors and airmen who fought and died. Even the cheaper food and raw materials that were counted as the 'benefits of empire' came at the expense of unemployment at home for workers whose goods could not be sold to impoverished colonial producers. But this was not what the nationalist propaganda said. Only the cartoonists revealed the truth, and on one occasion in 1941 caused a parliamentary furore during the German U boat campaign, when an Evening Standard cartoon depicted a sailor on a raft in a stormy sea over the caption 'The price of petrol has been raised by a penny (official)'. More telling still was the cartoon of Europe's foreign ministers in 1914 depicting them as crocodiles weeping tears over the aggressive instincts of their peoples. We shall have to bear in mind such insights as we look at the rise and fall of Yugoslavia.

History and nationality

The two essays which follow take the form of reviews. The first considers the thesis of Misha Glenny, one of the most respected journalists to cover the early years of the war in Yugoslavia and one of the most influential writers on the causes of the war. I have followed the historical direction which he has given to his book in calling it the 'Third Balkan War'.* It is impossible to understand the Yugoslav socialist experiment except in the context of the country's history, although I think that Glenny's history is fatally flawed. The first essay is therefore largely

---

*Misha Glenny, *The Fall of Yugoslavia: the Third Balkan War*, Penguin, 1993, p.258.

historical. I have taken into account other writings which follow Glenny's thesis that the collapse of Yugoslavia was inevitable, once Tito was dead and the central military power was weakened which, it is argued, was all that had ever held together the diverse ethnic groups.

It may surprise some readers that I have given rather little direct attention to the outpourings of those who have sought support for one or other of the nationalist leaders in ex-Yugoslavia. Whether they come from Croat nationalists like Branka Magaš, supporters of Serbian nationalists like Carl Jacobsen, or of the Muslim nationalists like Norman Cigar, their views are so one-sided as to be quite unhelpful in discovering the truth. The central theme of my two essays is not to blame or acclaim any one of the nationalist forces which broke up Yugoslavia, but to condemn all forms of nationalism. Name-calling does nobody any good. I should not perhaps have called Tudjman's regime in Croatia 'fascist', but the flag it flies is the same as that which went into battle side by side with the German iron cross and swastika. Branka Magaš should not have called the Yugoslav Communist Party between 1941 and 1945 'Stalinist in formation and mentality.' Neither Croats nor Serbs should call Bosnian Moslems 'Turks'. But then, if we are making moral judgements: Serbs should not have driven tens of thousands of Moslems out of Eastern Bosnia, and Croats should not have driven tens of thousands of Serbs out of Krajina; Serbs should not have bombed Sarajevo and Croats should not have destroyed the Moslem half of Mostar; a Moslem should not have founded the first nationalist party in Bosnia, and so on and so on. We have to discover why all these terrible things happened.

This is what I try to do in my second essay where I seek to show how the link between socialism and nationalism has to be explored. I have approached the subject by way of a kind of running commentary on two recent books by the same author, Susan Woodward of the United States' Brookings Institution.

THE YUGOSLAV TRAGEDY

This has three advantages: first, it gives authority to those judgements of mine which agree with hers; second, where we disagree, I am engaging with an exceptionally well-informed and intelligent mind; third, it seems likely that her books will become standard works on the subject for some time, and I do not think that they should rest unchallenged in certain quite important respects. There are valuable lessons to be learnt from the Yugoslav experience, but I do not think they can be contained within the assumptions from which Susan Woodward* starts her analysis. This is the first sentence of her second book:

> 'On the eve of the 1989 revolutions in eastern and central Europe, Yugoslavia was better poised than any other socialist country to make a successful transition to a market economy and to the West. It had after all been moving toward full global integration since its Communist Party leadership broke with Stalin in 1948.'

I do not accept the assumption that this was a possible or desirable transition or integration. I shall have to indicate why as I go along, and I will need to suggest in the process what alternatives there might be, or have been. At the same time, I have no doubt that Susan Woodward has written by far the best books so far on the Yugoslav tragedy. They are long books and sometimes hard work. The division of the subject by themes rather than by historical sequence makes for some repetition and the argument is often dense, but nobody who wants to understand what happened in Yugoslavia, not only since 1990 but in the previous five decades can afford not to read these books.

Susan Woodward writes with authority. A senior fellow in the Foreign Policy Studies programme at the Brookings Institution

---

*Susan L. Woodward, *Balkan Tragedy: Chaos and Dissolution after the Cold War*, Brookings Institution, Washington, 1995, pp.536, 1995, pb., 0815795149, distributed in the UK by Estover, Plymbridge, Devon.

Susan L. Woodward, *Socialist Unemployment: The Political Economy of Yugoslavia, 1945-1990*, Princeton University Press, 1995, pp.443, pb., distributed in the UK by Chichester, Wiley.

(for English readers, the equivalent of Chatham House), she worked for some years in Yugoslavia, has a perfect command of the Serbo-Croatian languages and was for most of 1994 senior adviser to Yasushi Akashi, the top UN official in the former Yugoslavia and special representative of UN Secretary General Boutros Boutros-Ghali. Her two long books perfectly complement each other. The first on Yugoslavia's political economy from 1945 to 1990 establishes the main weaknesses of the Yugoslav economic system and the way economic reforms required by Western creditors had begun to undermine the power of governments in Yugoslavia, as they did elsewhere. The second could not have been written without the first. It analyses the dissolution of the federation after 1991 and reveals the desperate struggle of nationalist leaders in the successor states to gain power and to hold on to it, bidding for international support with every means at their disposal.

Unfortunately, there is one weakness which Woodward's books share with Glenny's. Neither of them shows any appreciation of the extraordinary success of the war-time struggle for national liberation in the social liberation and the uniting of the Yugoslav peoples. Glenny can see the years 1941-1945 only as a war between Yugoslavs, because he believes that it is in age-long internicine hatred re-emerging after Tito's death that are to be found the causes of Yugoslavia's fall and the horrific killings that accompanied it. Woodward cannot see the years 1941-1945 except in relation to her main thesis of the widening gap between the more developed republics of the north-west and the underdeveloped south. Thus the war-time resistance of Slovenia was cut off from the rest of the Partisan armies. Croatia came late into the struggle after the Germans had successfully established a puppet Croat state. What she misses is the unity that was achieved. Kardelj and Kidrich and many others worked for Yugoslavia, not just for Croatia. But she misses something else more important; the social liberation that was achieved of whole peoples from the historic condition of an illiterate, oppressed and backward peasantry.

It is very hard now perhaps for those who have only seen the horror of the war in Bosnia to believe that there was so much of good in the Yugoslavia that has been destroyed. I can only say to them that there are still towns and villages where two or three national groups continue to live together. Tusla remains a multi-national city. In 1994 the young people went out onto the streets there in their thousands to celebrate Tito's birthday. Journalists who reject all forms of nationalism have come together since 1992 to establish a network of internal communication between all the old republics and regions (AIM — Alternative Information Media) and to inform the outside world that the nationalists have not won the hearts and minds of many millions of people who still think of themselves as Yugoslavs. These men and women wherever they are, in their homes or forced out of them, sometimes beyond the old Yugoslav boundaries, still look back with a deep sense of bereavement to a happy land of brothers and sisters. That is the measure of what has been destroyed by nationalism, which has ever been the instrument that the great powers have used to divide and conquer.

II

The Question of a
Third Balkan War

Understanding the Yugoslav tragedy is of enormous importance for the future of Europe, for what was the Soviet Union and indeed for other parts of the world where different nations live within one state. If we fail to understand and to learn lessons from this tragedy, we shall see the experience repeated over and over again with the same bloody results. The chapter which follows starts from a review of the two most popular studies of the fall of Yugoslavia and the awful conflict in Bosnia.* My long connection with Yugoslavia, which reaches back rather more than fifty years, leads me to question the explicit assumptions of both these studies (a) that what has happened is the end result of a long history of ethnic difference; and (b) that the 'West' has been guilty of not intervening militarily to prevent the bloodshed.

'Bloody Bosnia'
It is necessary to go back a long way into European history to understand the differences in Bosnia; and the *Guardian*/Channel 4 booklet tries to do this. But it is quite false to call them ethnic or even religious divisions; all the people are Slavs who speak the same language and regard their religious difference in terms of historic nationality. Their differences have in the past led to bloodshed and massacre, but at no time in history has this been on anything even approaching the horrendous nature and scale

---

*Misha Glenny, *The Fall of Yugoslavia: the Third Balkan War*, Penguin, 1993, p.258.

Noll Scott & Derek Jones (eds.) *Bloody Bosnia: a European Tragedy*, *Guardian* & Channel 4, 1993, pp.50.

of the violence of the last three years. Past outbreaks of violence have generally been a response to external invaders — Hungarian, Turkish, Italian, German — inciting one nationality against another, to divide and conquer; never before has the origin been so very largely internal. There is something missing in the so-called 'ethnic' explanations.

What is totally missing from both these studies is a single word about the catastrophic economic condition to which the country had been reduced, not by the war, but prior to Yugoslavia's collapse. While both books are fairly even-handed in the blame they assign respectively to the Croat and Serbian leaders for the emergence of a virulent nationalism which led to the dismemberment of Bosnia, the reasons for this nationalistic outbreak are not examined. There is no mention of the growing inequalities of incomes between the northern republics — Slovenia and Croatia — and the south including Bosnia, or of the huge disparity between the condition of those who had access to *deutschmarks* and those who had only *dinars*, which by 1989 were depreciating at hyper-inflationary rates.

If we do not understand the basic facts of the results of debt and inflation, we shall not be prepared for the next internecine horror. Like Yugoslavia in Europe, Somalia had the highest level of debt to national income of any country in Africa, and almost in the world. Among the 25 countries with the highest foreign debts in the 1980s, we find not only Chad, Mozambique, Somalia, Sudan, Uganda, Iraq, Israel, Turkey, Bolivia, Colombia, Guatemala, Nicaragua, Peru, Philippines, Myanmar, Indonesia, where civil wars are still raging or have just ceased, but also Algeria, Mexico, Nigeria where they are just starting, and what should we say of India and one-time Soviet Union?

Martin Woollacott in his contribution to the *Guardian* booklet chides the governments of the West and their peoples for 'their refusal to contemplate real risks and sacrifices by using or credibly threatening the use of force . . . misusing their troops as grocery boys while opposing any American action that might lead to fighting.' He contrasts this failure with the Gulf War where 'international institutions seemed to have proved their value, national governments had demonstrated their resolve, and military forces had stunningly demonstrated their capacities'. On this analogy, Milosevic would still be Serbia's dictator (Tudjman likewise in Croatia) but there would be 100,000 more Serbian soldiers dead (and Croats too) together with untold numbers of civilian casualties, the whole infrastructure of Serbia and Bosnia (and presumably of Croatia) — roads, railways, bridges, electricity and water supplies, tele-communications and government buildings — would be destroyed and the Albanians, like the Kurds, in process of decimation. What was left of Bosnia would, like Kuwait, have been 'rescued' to return to a totally undemocratic regime.

What neither Martin Woollacott nor any of the other contributors to *Bloody Bosnia* mention is the real responsibility of the West first in the demand of the banks for debt repayment, which as elsewhere led to rising inflation; and second, in Chancellor Kohl's recognition of the withdrawal from Yugoslavia of the two rich republics — Slovenia and then Croatia. Recognition of Croatia was much the more serious because, while Slovenia has a largely homogeneous population of Slovenes with their own language and historic links with Austria, Croatia has large Serbian populations in Slavonia and in Krajina and a large Croat population in Bosnia. Recognition without guarantees for Serbian minorities and without any limit set to Croat ambitions in Bosnia was bound to result in a Yugoslav army led by Serbs entering Croatian and Bosnian territory; and then there could be no limit to the grab for territory until Bosnia was divided up between Serbia and Croatia.

National hatred

Misha Glenny's book is much more ambitious than the *Guardian* booklet. It shares the same brilliance of the eye-witness accounts of the war, which Maggie O'Kane and Ed Vulliamy contribute to *Bloody Bosnia*. But Misha Glenny has tried to probe more deeply — to understand a country whose fate Bosnia's most famous modern writer foretold in the following words of premonition seventy years ago:

'And just as there are mineral riches under the earth in Bosnia, so undoubtedly are Bosnians rich in hidden moral values, which are more rarely found in their compatriots in other Yugoslav lands. But . . . there's one thing that the people of Bosnia . . . must realise and never lose sight of — Bosnia is a country of hatred and fear . . . the fatal characteristic of this hatred is that the Bosnian man is unaware of the hatred that lives in him, shrinks from analysing it — and hates everyone who tries to do so. And yet it's a fact that in Bosnia and Herzegovina there are more people ready in fits of this subconscious hatred to kill and be killed, for different reasons, and under different pretexts, than in other much bigger Slav and non-Slav lands . . .

. . . it can also be said that there are few countries with such firm belief, elevated strength of character, so much tenderness and loving passion, such depth of feeling, of loyalty and unshakeable devotion, or with such a thirst for justice. But in secret depths underneath all this hide burning hatreds, entire hurricanes of tethered and compressed hatreds maturing and awaiting their hour. Those who oppress and exploit the economically weaker do it with hatred into the bargain, which makes the exploitation a hundred times harder and uglier; while those who bear these injustices dream of justice and reprisal, but as some explosion of vengeance which, if it were realised according to their ideas, would perforce be so complete that it would blow to pieces the oppressed along with the hated oppressors.'

Ivo Andric, *A Letter from 1920*, in Celia Hawkesworth's edition of Andric's short stories, published by Forest Books, London and Dereta, Belgrade, 1992

A new edition of Misha Glenny's *Fall of Yugoslavia* brings his story of the war in Yugoslavia up to June of 1993, when the carve up of Bosnia between Serb and Croat armed forces was being completed. It was then largely in the hands of the UN negotiators what would be left for the remaining Moslem population to live in. But Misha Glenny's book is subtitled 'The Third Balkan War', and if that is not a journalistic flourish, and it should not be, then his belief is that there is more trouble to come. We are all influenced by where we live. Glenny lives in Thessaloniki in northern Greece, when he is not travelling as the BBC's central European correspondent based on Vienna. So, he will have a lively awareness of warlike alarums in the Balkan peninsula, and of the Greek peoples' fears of what is happening on their northern border. I believe that Glenny's warnings are well taken; the book is a brilliant and courageous story from a war correspondent, but his analysis of the Yugoslav problem is deeply flawed. We have to understand the problem in a much wider setting.

The Balkan wars and the great powers
The first two Balkan wars were fought in 1912 and 1913. They were about the partition not of Yugoslavia but of Macedonia and Albania. In the first war, Bulgaria, Serbia, Montenegro and Greece united to end Turkish rule in what remained of the Ottoman empire. In this they succeeded far beyond their expectations, driving the Turks back to Constantinople. The second war followed, when Bulgaria sought to take more of Macedonia than the Greeks and Serbs would permit and Romania entered the fray to seize Bulgarian lands where Romanians lived south of the Danube. The Bulgarian armies besieged from all sides were heavily defeated. Greece and Serbia divided up Macedonia between them, and Turkey regained lost ground around Adrianople. Albania which had been occupied by both Greece and Serbia was declared by the great powers to be an independent state, and the Greeks and Serbs had to leave.

Behind all this fighting lay the rivalries of the great European powers, which one year later were to break out into open warfare, when the Archduke Ferdinand of Austria was murdered in Sarajevo. What were then the interests of the great powers in the Balkans and what are they today? We need to know because much of the thinking about national interests which determines policy in the chancelleries of Europe has a long history.

It had always been traditional British policy to maintain control of the Mediterranean and particularly to keep Russia away from the sea routes to India. It probably still is. It dates back to the carve up of Europe at the Treaty of Utrecht in 1713. Britain, having decisively defeated France and Spain in a war for the succession to the Holy Roman Empire, turned away from Europe to build an empire overseas. The defeat had to be repeated a century later, but significantly it had to be at sea. By the treaty of Utrecht, the Netherlands, Italy and the Mediterranean islands had passed from Spanish to Austrian rule. Above all, the monopoly of the slave trade passed from Spain to Britain. Austria was not a maritime or commercial power, so could be trusted with possessions along the great trade routes. She could even be encouraged to look south-east for an empire; and by 1718 had occupied Hungary, Croatia and parts of Serbia across the Danube.

At the same time, the British wished to set a limit to this expansion as well as to Russian expansion southwards. The Turks provided this. Their Ottoman Empire spread right across the Balkans. But, throughout the Nineteenth Century, Turkey was an ailing power and it became necessary for the Ottoman empire to be bolstered up. Although popular opinion in Britain supported the independence movements against Turkish rule, first in Serbia and then in the Greek War of Independence in 1820, Turkish power was supported by western governments. The disastrous Crimean war of 1854-5 was fought to try to stop Russia's southward expansion and her exercise of battleships through the Black Sea.

At that time, France and Austria supported the British, but within a dozen years a new power had arrived on the scene, when in 1866 Prussian arms defeated Austria at Sadowa in Bohemia and, in 1871, a newly united Germany destroyed the armies of France. Bismarck had neutralised Russia by promising to support the opening of the Black Sea straits to the Russian navy. Britain and France moved inexorably into alliance with each other and then, very uneasily, with Russia against the greater danger of a German drive to the East. Germany entered into alliance with Austria in 1879, and, in the meantime, Austria had extended her hold on the Balkans by the occupation of Bosnia-Herzegovina. Alliance with Turkey was necessary for Germany for the next stage of the Berlin-Baghdad railway to advance Germany's eastern ambitions.

Thus by 1913, the line up of the great powers in the Balkans was already clear. Britain had failed to keep the Russian navy locked up in the Black Sea but was determined to keep a firm hold on the Mediterranean. This meant an independent Albania and Greece and agreement with a newly liberated and unified Italy to maintain the status quo. Russia supported her southern Slav brothers — particularly the Serbs — but also Bulgaria as a weapon against the Turks, who were driven into the arms of Germany. In close alliance with Russia stood France. Together, Austria and Hungary, united by their fear of Russia, controlled the Danube, maintaining an alliance with Romania, despite her rule over Hungarians in Trans-Sylvania, and sought at all costs to keep Serbia as small as possible. The murder of the Austrian emperor's son and heir in Sarajevo provided the German army with the excuse, probably planned in advance, for mobilisation in support of Austria's attack on Belgrade.

When Germany was defeated after four years of murderous trench warfare in France and Belgium, the treaty of Versailles opened up that 'prison house of nations', the Austro-Hungarian Empire. But a south-Slav state — Yugoslavia — was created under a Serbian king for the Slovenes, Croats, Serbs, Montenegrins and the peoples of Bosnia-Herzegovina and Vardar Macedonia. How far were they in fact separate nations? The southern Slavs had settled peacefully in the region in the

Seventh Century; but they had been cut off from the northern Slavs by the irruption of Magyars into what is now Hungary, by the presence of the Vlachs, called Romanians because of their origins in the Roman province of Dacia, from which they retained their Latin tongue, and by the Bolgars, a Mongol people like the Magyars, but who, unlike the Magyars, abandoned their language for a Slavonic tongue.

The Southern Slavs

All the south Slavs have a similar language, but they had very dissimilar histories. The Slovenes had never formed a political state, but, while they were the most westernised, had a long history of struggle against both Italy and Austria. The Croats had a kingdom from 900 to 1100, which was rival to Venice on the Dalmatian coast, until they were conquered by the king of Hungary. Croatia remained a province of Hungary, with a certain autonomy, until 1918, even providing the general who helped to put down the revolution of 1848. But the Hungarians relied on Serbian garrisons in what is called the *vojna krajina* (military frontier) against Bosnia to the south. An independent kingdom had been established in Bosnia too during the eleventh and twelfth centuries, but it then fell under Ottoman ascendancy. Serbia had the most long lasting empire, continuing from 1168 to 1496 (what Magaš calls 'a short lived empire'). However, after the defeat of a combined Serbian army by the Turks at Kosovo in 1389, the Serbs were brought increasingly under Hungarian rule in the north and Turkish rule in the south. Large numbers of Serbs, especially the landowning class, embraced the faith of their conquerors to retain possession of their property. Their serfs and peasants followed suit.

The field of Kosovo, despite Serbia's defeat, remains the most sacred site in Serbian folk memory and the fact that it is today largely occupied by Albanians makes it the flash-point for new wars. Milosevic has already used the appeal to Kosovo as the rallying cry of Serbian nationalism. Yet for over five hundred years mixed south Slav populations of Christians and Moslems, including Albanians, have lived together in relative peace until today. This is the more remarkable in Bosnia because the Christians themselves are divided between Catholic and Orthodox.

Even before the lands which now form Bosnia and Herzegovina were divided between Hungarian and Turkish rule, the great schism of the eastern and western empires of Rome ran down through the middle of Bosnia from the Danube and the river Drava in the north to what is now Dubrovnik (Ragusa) in the south. This then became the line that divided Catholic from Orthodox Christendom and later set the northern limit to the empire that the Turks could hold against Hungarians and Austrians.

What kept Bosnia together in the past

Bosnia has thus been a battleground over the centuries between separate Christian faiths, between Moslem and Christian, and between separate empires, Austro-Hungarian and Ottoman, not to mention the influence of Venice on the west and Russia on the east. By their geographical position the Croats embraced Catholicism and the Serbs Orthodoxy. How did Bosnia survive? The answer that Misha Glenny gives is central to his explanation of what is happening today, and is worth quoting in full:

'Bosnia has always survived by dint of a protective shield provided either by a Yugoslav state or the Austrian or Ottoman empires. Of all the entities making up former Yugoslavia, Bosnia boasts the longest history as a definable state, kingdom or republic. Nonetheless its internal stability was invariably guaranteed by an external power which mediated between the three communities (the sublime Porte, Vienna, the inter-war royal dictatorship or Titoism). On the one occasion that this broke down between 1941 and 1945, the results were horrifying: a nationalist, religious war whose violence surpassed that of all other wartime conflicts in the region.'

THE YUGOSLAV TRAGEDY

(Glenny, p.144) (note: the 'sublime Porte' was the name given to the Ottoman capital of Constantinople.)

I believe this explanation of Glenny's to be profoundly wrong on two counts. The first is that all the so-called 'mediating external powers' sedulously practised the arts of divide and conquer. This did not always work. After 1918, Serbs and Croats sought a united state and, in 1938, came together in protest at the royal dictatorship. The second count is that the Yugoslav national liberation struggle between 1941 and 1945 against German and Italian occupation cannot by any stretching of the meaning of words be described as 'a nationalist, religious war'. It is true that appalling crimes were committed by the Croat fascist Ustashe at Kozara and Jasenovac in 1942, with German connivance. The numbers murdered amounted at a conservative estimate to some 200,000 Serbs, Jews and Gypsies; some say a million. It is also true that atrocities were committed by Serbs against those they believed to be traitors. But Croats and Serbs fought side by side against the Germans and Italians.

The National Liberation Movement of Yugoslavia, 1941-45

The war between 1941 and 1945 in Yugoslavia was, in very truth, a war in which Yugoslavs of all national origins and religious faiths fought against German, Austrian and Italian armies. The number of Croat Ustashe and other local forces fighting on the side of the Axis powers was negligible and Glenny himself admits that Croat forces were largely responsible for their own liberation. Yet he refers throughout the book to the 'Serb-dominated Partisans'. This is a phrase that gives a totally false impression to anyone who is ignorant of the nature of the Yugoslav national liberation struggle during those years, which united the people against a common enemy and provided credibility to what Glenny calls the 'protective shield of "Titoism"'.

To start with, Tito was himself a Croat. The majority of his generals certainly were Serbs or Montenegrins, but of the first rank, those who fought in the Spanish civil war, Peko Dabcevic was a Montenegrin, Koca Popovic was a Serb, Kosta Nadj and Ivo Rukavina were Croats, and Rozman was a Slovene; Apostolski was a Macedonian. Of Tito's closest associates in 1943, Zujovic and Rankovic were Serbs, Djilas and Dabcevic were Montenegrins, Kardelj was a Slovene, Dr. Ribar, the President of AVNOJ (Anti-fascist Council of National Liberation), was a Croat (his two sons held important posts before they were killed in battle) and Mosha Pijade was a Jew. It was a broad mix of the nationalities in command. Glenny insists that it was mainly Serbs including Montenegrins who died in Tito's armies. If that is true, it is not surprising. There were more of them in the total population and on account of the mountainous location of guerrilla warfare, it was mostly Montenegrins and south Serbs who were caught in the German offensives against the Partisan strongholds.

Noel Malcolm in his *Bosnia: a Short History* provides some support for Glenny's view that the 1941-45 war in Yugoslavia was primarily a war between Yugoslavs. He seeks first to build up the strength of the Chetnik forces under Mihailovic, who was an ex-Royal Yugoslav army commander, and dates their first collaboration with the Germans as late as September 1943 — that is after the Italian surrender, which delivered great quantities of arms into Partisan hands. The fact is that the Chetniks were fighting alongside the Germans during the Fourth German offensive in March of 1943, when the Partisans succeeded in escaping from a German-Chetnik pincer movement at the River Neretva and in driving the Chetniks into Montenegro. Malcolm shows no sign of having read the official record on the British decision to switch support from Mihailovic to Tito, which predates Chetnik collaboration to long before 1943 (Auty, P. and

THE YUGOSLAV TRAGEDY

Clogg, R. (eds), *British Wartime Policy towards Resistance in Yugoslavia and Greece*, 1975).

Malcolm further denies that Tito's forces ever pinned down any large number of German divisions, asserting that

> 'at the beginning of 1943 there were only four German divisions, of low calibre, in the whole of Yugoslavia. (In August of that year they were joined by two reserve divisions of trainee recruits, and one burnt-out division from Stalingrad; and a few more were brought in towards the end of the year after the surrender of Italian forces in September) . . .'

How many was 'a few more'? On January 18, 1944, Sir James Grigg, British War Minister told the House of Commons:

> 'The Partisan army has at one time or another during this period engaged up to fifteen German divisions which might otherwise have been profitably employed elsewhere.'

The crucial issue relates to the period just before the Allied landings in France, when Prime Minister Churchill himself informed the House of Commons that the Partisans'

> 'guerrilla army of over a quarter of a million men . . . is holding in check fourteen out of the twenty German divisions in the Balkan Peninsula, in addition to six Bulgarian divisions and other satellite forces'.

There really can be no question that the war in Yugoslavia between 1941 an 1945 was a war of national liberation that involved all the Yugoslav peoples in the struggle against Axis occupation. To return to Misha Glenny, the crucial question for him relates to the condition of Bosnia immediately after the Germans and Italians had been driven out. It was my job to travel throughout Bosnia and Herzegovina, following up the German withdrawal. There was much destruction, especially of bridges and houses near to important communications of road and rail, but most of the towns and larger villages were standing and in them the usual mix of catholic church, orthodox church and mosque, generally more than one of each, all damaged but not destroyed. There are two points to notice: first, they are not standing now; second, there were mixed national/religious communities in most of Bosnia's towns and larger villages.

The drawing up of maps to reveal the so-called 'ethnic distribution' in Bosnia, begun in the Vance-Owen plan and perpetuated by others (e.g Branka Magaš, *The Destruction of Yugoslavia*, 'Table of Ethnic Composition', p.18 and map of 'National and Ethnic Distribution' on p.178 and the map of so-called 'Ethnic Yugoslavia' in *Bloody Bosnia*, p.11), gives a totally misleading impression. Firstly, there are no ethnic divisions among Slavs and, secondly, the areas marked 'Serb' or 'Croat' or 'Muslim' on these maps of Bosnia-Herzegovina are only areas where there *was* a majority of one or the other of the three national/religious communities. There *were* virtually no enclaves of any one group. One has to say 'was' and 'were' because 'ethnic cleansing' has made the maps on paper into a terrible reality on the ground today.

If the mutual antagonism of the separate peoples of Bosnia has boiled up into something far worse than at any earlier period of history, leading to mass murder, 'ethnic cleansing' and the destruction of houses, churches and mosques on a scale far greater than even the German 'scorched earth' policy, then there must be another explanation than that of settling past scores. Glenny sees the war in Bosnia-Herzegovina as 'a continuation of the struggle between 1941 and 1945 . . . a revival of unresolved conflicts, prejudices and vendettas on a local level.' (pp.147-8) He goes on:

'The conflict inside Yugoslavia between 1941 and 1945 assumed such bloody proportions that, were it ever to revive, it was always likely to be merciless. . . . the wars of the Yugoslav succession have been nationalist in character. They are not ethnic conflicts . . . what is striking about Bosnia-Herzegovina, in particular, is just how closely related are the Serbs, the Croats and the Moslems. Religion is the crucial factor dividing these people, although this is not a confessional conflict. For centuries, these people have been asked to choose between competing empires and ideologies, which have been invariably defined by religion.' (pp.171-2)

There is obviously some truth in this distinction between so-called 'ethnic' divisions and those derived from historical and religious associations. But it is simply not possible to describe in this way the war of national liberation from 1941 to 1945. And since then, religion has not prevented one quarter of all Yugoslav marriages from crossing the religious divide, whether between Catholic and Orthodox or Christian and Moslem. Glenny never mentions this most significant fact, nor the fact that in the 1981 census more than one in ten of the population of Bosnia and also of Croatia recorded their nationality as Yugoslav, and not as Serb or Croatian. Since Glenny sees the war in Yugoslavia primarily as a religious war, the Moslems in Bosnia have to be seen by him primarily as a religious grouping, but that is not the reality.

The Bosnian Moslems

It is of crucial importance to understand the meaning of the statement that some one-time Yugoslavs are Moslems. Under the 1974 Yugoslav Constitution, Moslems had gained the right to use a capital 'M' in official documents, as a recognised Yugoslav nationality, but it did not make them particularly religious. Islamic fundamentalism has never taken root in Bosnia or elsewhere in ex-Yugoslavia, although President Izetbegovic was jailed for publishing *Theses on an Islamic State*. When war broke out, Bosnians became either Serbs or Croats or Moslems, but fundamentalist volunteers from the Middle East who came to fight were not welcomed. Glenny seeks to emphasise the rise of Moslem consciousness before 1989 because he sees the Moslems as another nationalistic force. He recognises the historic importance of Izetbegovic being the first of the Bosnian leaders to organise a political party, the SDA (Moslem), on nationalist lines in 1990. But, it is doubtful whether this then reflected a rising Moslem consciousness; most Moslems desired no such development.

Glenny traces Moslem fear of the Serbs back to the struggle for liberation. In talking of the impact of the Second World War as 'a genocidal struggle between Serbs and Croats . . . felt most keenly in Bosnia' he writes that 'The majority of Moslems co-operated with the Croat fascists, the Ustashas, against the Serb-dominated Partisans.' He admits that 'in some areas, like the north-western enclave of Casin-Bihac', support for the Partisans was much stronger among the Moslems'. (p.140) But, this was not an enclave in any sense of an area of foreign territory; and the general view that 'the majority of Moslems co-operated with the Croat fascists' cannot be supported.

Certainly, the majority of the Moslem *leaders* threw in their lot in 1942 with the puppet government of Pavelic, but many later deserted to the Partisans. Most of the rich merchants and landowners undoubtedly collaborated, but from their sons who had gone to university, especially those who went to Paris, was drawn a high proportion of the political commissars with the Partisans.

The fact is that the attitude of the majority of Moslems in Bosnia-Herzegovina throughout the national liberation struggle was one not of collaboration, but of withdrawal to avoid trouble. Most of the Moslem population, of course, were neither landowners nor merchants, but peasants and craftsmen. The Partizans were successful in the fighting against the German armies in Bosnia, where most of the major battles took place, primarily because they were disciplined and never looted and followed the rule that 'those who are not against us are for us'. It was well known that there were many Moslem women who helped the Partizans, while their men were in hiding or had been enrolled to fight alongside the Axis.

Glenny's characterisation of the Moslems' role in the war leads him to make what is, I believe, a further error in relation to the position of the Moslems under Tito's industrialisation of Bosnia for war purposes. He writes:

'The poorly educated Moslem artisan classes were rapidly transformed into a literate working class, while the ambitious educational programme of the Communist Party unwittingly encouraged the development of a Moslem intelligentsia, as it did an Albanian and Macedonian intelligentsia . . . The student unrest which swept Europe in 1968 found a powerful resonance in Sarajevo . . . As latent nationalist tension between Serbs and Croats within the Yugoslav League of Communists emerged into the open, for the first time since the war, between 1966 and 1972, Moslem functionaries in the Bosnian League of Communists successfully applied pressure on the leadership in Belgrade to elevate the Moslem's status from national minority to constituent nation.' (p.141)

Again, there is some truth in this, although why Communist Party education should be 'unwitting' is not explained. But the main point is that, while there was a small number of craftsmen who could be recruited for industrialisation, most of the Moslems who entered the new factories in Bosnia were peasants whose farms were uneconomic. Sociological studies in the 1970s revealed that many became alienated, took to drinking and became an 'under-class', which suffered badly when the economy went into decline in the 1980s after the years of boom. Moslem resentment in Bosnia in the 1970s can better be understood in class terms than in nationalist or religious terms. It was, of course, convenient for the Communist League to divert class struggles into other channels. We need only to remember the warning from Ivo Andric to recognise how easily that could be done.

The real explanation: 'the economy, stupid!'

This brings us, at length, to the real explanation for the fratricidal killings in Bosnia. If people who had lived together in relative peace for so long, in spite of national and religious differences, and had mainly fought side by side in the struggle for liberation from Axis occupation in 1941-45, could descend to mass murder, there must be something that happened in the 1980s to open up Pandora's box of hatred. There was something; it was the state of the economy. The extraordinary thing about Misha Glenny's book is that this something finds not a word of mention. Yet, what happened was nothing less than the total and catastrophic collapse of the Yugoslav economy. [This question is dealt with in the chapter that follows.]

The role of the great powers today

We have, then, to understand the economic background to Milosevic's 'Great Serb' ambitions, to Tudjman's Croat nationalism, to Moslem nationalism and to the emergence of the fascists and thugs, football fan leaders, criminals and gangsters who came out of the woodwork as the whole structure of Yugoslav society fell apart. It cannot be by chance that the country in Europe with the highest proportion of foreign debt to national income was Yugoslavia, and in Africa was Somalia. In both countries, the young men toting their AK 47s may come from disturbed childhoods and backgrounds of tribal hatred, but the occasion for their emergence must be the breakdown of their societies. When all hope of escape from declining living standards disappears, when the harder you work, the more you export and the less you earn with a continuously deteriorating currency, or when you are unemployed and others are doing well, then it must be your neighbour's fault. He has *deutschmarks* or better land or friends in power, and if his name is a Moslem one or a Croat one and yours is Serbian, it does not need a Radovan Karadjic to tell you what to do.

But the real criminals are not in Yugoslavia at all. They are, as before, in the chancelleries of the European powers, where they refuse to write off the debts of the poor countries but only those of their own bankers, and where they plot the future of the Balkan peoples to suit their own long term interests. The authors of *Bloody Bosnia* write of 'Tito winning billions of Western dollars to prop up his own brand of communism . . .' The fact is that they were borrowed dollars and had to be repaid with interest. At the same time, world-wide interest rates rose, the world price of Yugoslav raw material exports fell and the country had to export more and more manufactured goods to fill the gap.

One point that saves Misha Glenny's book, apart from the quite extraordinary courage he showed in travelling through war torn ex-Yugoslavia to report what he saw, is his condemnation of Chancellor Kohl for forcing upon the European Community the recognition of Croatia. This was despite the report of Judge Robert Badinter, President of the French Constitutional Court, in which it was made clear that the rights of minorities in Croatia were not guaranteed and his warning that claims to the lands occupied by Croats inside Bosnia were still being made by the Croat nationalist leaders.

Once Croatia's independence was recognised, with no guarantees for the large Serbian minorities within Croatia's borders, war between Serbs and Croats was assured inside Croatia; but, even worse, this war would be bound to spread to Bosnia, which each would seek to divide between them at the expense of the Moslems. It need not have happened, and it would not have happened, but for the collapse of Yugoslavia's economy and the special interests of a German Chancellor. For, Chancellor Kohl depends for his majority in the German Parliament on the Catholic voters for the Christian party in Bavaria. This is a party with historic ties to the Catholics in Austria, Hungary, Slovenia and Croatia. The Pope himself blessed these ties just before the day of Croat recognition.

One might take a still longer historical view of the question and ask whether a once more united Germany, moving towards union with Austria in an expanded European Community, might not be wondering about control over the oil supplies of the Near East by way of direct access to the Adriatic. It is said that

Chancellor Kohl only obtained the support of Prime Minister Major for Croat recognition, by helping him with the defence of sterling and the Social Chapter opt-out. The British Foreign Office was opposed. Perhaps, it had recalled its traditional fear of Russia in the eastern Mediterranean. Foreign Secretary Douglas Hurd's defence of Serbia, in defiance of all the anti-Serb bias in the British media, can only have been from fear that Serbia should fall back into the arms of her old ally, Russia.

These speculations become important when we turn our eyes southwards, to the Macedonians and Albanians. The Macedonians are still divided between Bulgaria, Greece and the Macedonian republic of old Yugoslavia. The latter is slowly gathering recognition from the international community, but lacks European Community support because of the opposition of Greece. It is the 400,000 Albanians in (ex-Yugoslav) Macedonia that pose the main problem; for, Albanians too are divided between several countries — Greece as well as Kosovo, Macedonia and Serbia — where in total there are as many living outside Albania as there are in Albania itself. A united Albania is unacceptable to each of the three neighbouring states and has been vetoed by the United States. The same obstacle stands in the way of a united Macedonia. An American peace-keeping force is deployed in the region to maintain the status quo.

Misha Glenny is right to warn that an outbreak of fighting between Serbs and Moslems in the Sandjak Moslem majority enclave in Serbia or in Kosovo itself would be hard to stop from spreading throughout the region, and for once he recognises the danger resulting from collapsing economies — in this case those of Albania, Macedonia and Bulgaria. But the economic collapse in Serbia was just as serious. Popular protests in the south as well as the north led Milosevic in 1989 to occupy Kosovo as well as the Voyvodina, ending their autonomous status and even the cultural rights respectively of the Albanians and the Hungarians. This was just a part of the grab for territory by the nationalist leaders as Yugoslavia disintegrated, but it was not only in Bosnia that it seemed to threaten a wider conflagration. What Glenny sees from his home in Thessaloniki is a strongly reviving 'sick man of the Porte', presented with what he quotes Turgut Ozal describing as 'a once-in-a-lifetime opportunity for Turkey to restore its economic, diplomatic and cultural influence among Moslem vestiges of the Ottoman Empire' (pp.240-1). Glenny suggests that the United States would like to see a strong ally in the region, which could be relied upon to defend US interests in the neighbouring oil fields, without involving American soldiers; and Turkey perfectly fills the bill.

If it is United States policy in the Balkans to promote a role for Turkey, this would explain two recent positions taken up by the US. The first was to withdraw support from Kurdish claims against Saddam Hussein, since any independent Kurdish state would inevitably raise the question of the several million Kurds in Turkey. The second, and of much more significance for the Balkans, was the support given by President Clinton to the demand of Bosnia's Moslems for arms and even for armed intervention. There must be a suspicion that the pressure came from Turkey. Such an opening up of the Bosnian conflict could have provided Turkey with the credit for intervening on behalf of fellow Moslems. It must, however, be doubted whether Turkey would want to get deeply embroiled in the Balkans when it has even more pressing interests among the Turkish speaking peoples in the disintegrating Russian empire further east. Intervention in Bosnia was, in any case, strongly resisted by the Europeans; it would have only increased the fighting in Bosnia and spread it into the other Moslem communities — in the Sandjak, Kosovo and Macedonia.

European governments may well have been less concerned with the spread of fighting than with the re-entry of Russia behind the Serbian nationalists, and the recovery of Turkey as a major power in the most sensitive area of European interest — where the oil is — and a power which could no longer be relied upon, as in the Nineteenth Century, to do their bidding. In all this, Glenny may only be reflecting Greek paranoia, particuarly in Thessaloniki, at further evidence of the Turkish revival.

The message for the West European chancelleries if they want peace should not be to find ways to divide and conquer among the different interests in the region — British, German, Russian, Turkish, American — but rather to tackle seriously the task of achieving recovery in their own economies and with them the economic recovery of Eastern and Southern Europe. Debt remission should be a first step. It would be a small sacrifice for a larger gain, but payment would need to come from the investors and not from the taxpayers. In such steps towards income redistribution lie the only hopes for economic recovery and for peace. There seems to be little enough hope of this being recognised, but there is no way out of hatred except by some measure of contentment. 'For, what can war but endless war still breed?'

Works consulted

M. Barratt Brown, 'How the Debt Broke up Yugoslavia' in Ken Coates (ed.) *Drawing the Peace Dividend*, Spokesman, 1993.

Ken Coates and M. Barratt Brown, (eds.), *A European Recovery Programme*, Spokesman, 1993.

Basil Davidson, *Partisan Picture*, Bedford, 1946.

Vladimir Dedijer, *Tito Speaks*, Weidenfeld, 1953.

R.C.K. Ensor, *England 1870-1914*, Oxford, 1936.

H.A.L. Fisher, *A History of Europe*, Arnold, 1936.

Misha Glenny, *The Fall of Yugoslavia: the Third Balkan War*, Penguin, 1993.

Nevil Forbes et al., *The Balkans: A History*, Oxford, 1915.

Iraj Hashi, 'The Disintegration of Yugoslavia: Regional Disparities and the Nationalities Question', *Capital and Class*, no.48, Autumn, 1992.

Maja Korac, 'Women in the Balkan Wars', in Ken Coates (ed), *op.cit.*

Keesings, *Record of World Events*, vol 39, 1993 Reference Supplement.

Branka Magaš, *The Destruction of Yugoslavia*, Verso, 1993.

Noel Malcolm, *Bosnia: A Short History*, Macmillan 1994.

THE YUGOSLAV TRAGEDY

J.A.R. Marriott, *The Eastern Question*, Oxford, 1917.

R.I. Moore, (ed.)*The Hamlyn Historical Atlas*, Book Club Ass., 1981.

P.I.C.M.E., *The National Liberation Movement of Yugoslavia*, Bari, 1944.

Noll Scott & Derek Jones (eds.), *Bloody Bosnia: A European Tragedy*, *Guardian* and Channel 4 Television, 1993.

Hugh Seton-Watson, *Eastern Europe Between the Wars: 1918-1941*, Cambridge, 1945.

Mark Thompson, *A Paper House: The Ending of Yugoslavia*, Vintage, 1992.

Doreen Warriner, *Revolution in Eastern Europe*, Turnstile, 1950.

III

Socialism and Nationalism

False views about the Yugoslav tragedy

So widespread in both official and popular understanding are the false views which are generally accepted about the war in Yugoslavia that it is necessary to clear these out of the way before we can begin to look at the society which preceded the breakdown after 1990. Susan Woodward's books challenge the most widely accepted explanation of Yugoslavia's dissolution (clearly expressed in Misha Glenny's *Fall of Yugoslavia*) that the ethnic rivalries in the country had only been suppressed over the centuries by the exercise of military power — Ottoman, Austro-Hungarian, German and finally that of Tito. When that went, all hell was let loose. Woodward quotes Tito saying to Averell Harriman at Kardelj's funeral in 1979, a year before his own death in 1980, 'After me there will be chaos'. I do not believe it was meant seriously. Tito had taken every possible precaution to ensure continuing unity. It is of crucial importance for future historians to know whether there was that famous twinkle in those blue eyes, as he said it. Will Mrs Harriman please tell us?

Woodward's books equally challenge the view, almost as widely held and in effect contrary, that the whole disaster was the result of Serbian aggression; a view most assiduously propagated by the Croat nationalists (see especially Branka Magaš' *Destruction of Yugoslavia* and Mark Thompson's *A Paper House*) and equally by the Moslem nationalists (see Norman Cigar's *Genocide in Bosnia*). But Woodward's books go much further in questioning the basic assumption of many like Neil Malcolm (*Bosnia: A Short History*) that a centrally planned socialist economy was bound to collapse in Yugoslavia as elsewhere in Eastern Europe.

Some reviewers, such as Richard Crampton in the *Times Literary Supplement* (2.11.95), have supposed from a cursory glance at Susan Woodward's first book that she is arguing that the peculiar Yugoslav system of workers' control in 'associated labour' led workers inevitably to choose always higher wages rather than investment in more employment, so that in the end unacceptable levels of unemployment destroyed the state. This is based on the hypothesis of Benjamin Ward (in the *American Economic Review*, 1958 and 1967), but Woodward rubbishes it. In fact, real wages went down just when unemployment was rising fastest. There *was* always an incomes policy, even sometimes a voluntary concern for one which the Party could appeal to among men and women 'associated in labour'. What Woodward shows is that so few in the whole country were 'associated'. That is the central point of her thesis.

I need here to declare an interest. I am perhaps bound to commend Woodward's books because she corroborates, from a position of far greater authority than mine, my own analysis which has been the object of some derision. My own view has always been that the dissolution of Yugoslavia and the bitter fighting that followed cannot be understood simply in terms of ancient ethnic differences or of Serbian aggression. Yugoslavia's foreign debt and the economic measures required by the IMF throughout the 1980s to reduce it had, I believed, to be at the centre of any explanation. This is what Croat nationalists like Branka Magaš called my 'bogey of the foreign debt'.

Here is what Woodward says in 'The Argument in Brief' of her book, *The Balkan Tragedy*, with which I am very largely in agreement:

SOCIALISM AND NATIONALISM

'The conflict is not a result of historical animosities and it is not a return
to the pre-communist past; it is the result of the politics of transforming a
socialist society to a market economy and democracy. A critical element
of this failure was economic decline, caused largely by a program intended
to resolve a *foreign debt crisis* [emphasis added]. More than a decade of
austerity and declining living standards corroded the social fabric and the
rights and securities that individuals and families had come to rely on.'

Yugoslavia's political and economic structure

The effects of heavy foreign debts and of the economic reforms
required by the IMF to obtain finance to meet debt repayments
were in Yugoslavia quite exceptionally aggravated by the political
and economic structure of the country. Politically, Yugoslavia
was a federation of six republics — Slovenia, Croatia,
Bosnia-Herzegovina, Serbia, Montenegro and Macedonia —
and two autonomous regions within the Serbian republic —
Voyvodina and Kosovo-Metohia. Apart from the Magyars in the
Voyvodina and the Albanians in Kosovo, all were southern Slav
peoples (Yugoslavs). Each represented different historic
communities, depending on the influence on them of their several
conquerors — Turks, Venetians, Austrians, Hungarians — and
on their religious conversions — Christian Catholic (mostly in
Slovenia and Croatia), Christian Orthodox (mostly in Serbia and
Montenegro), Moslem (mostly in Bosnia). No republic consisted
wholly of one community; the nearest to that was Slovenia.
Bosnia was the most mixed and, contrary to the understanding
of those who tried to draw up ethnic maps of provinces or cantons
for each group, nearly every one of the 110 districts of
Bosnia-Herzegovina contained two, and more often three,
different communities. Woodward's *Balkan Tragedy* has an
excellent map and statistical table to show this.

The Yugoslav constitution of 1946, revised in 1963 and 1974,
was based upon the equal rights of all peoples wherever they
lived, but it also established a federation of republics. Wherever
there were mixed communities, the *kljuc* (or national quota)

45

operated in appointments to positions in the social (public) sector, as it did in the federal government. After Tito's death, the presidency of the federation rotated around the republics. At first, the division of powers retained the 'commanding heights' of the economy — finance, foreign trade, heavy industry, transport and communications — as well as foreign affairs and defence at the centre. In successive constitutions more and more power was delegated to the republics and also to enterprises themselves.

Especially important, in the 1960s the state monopoly of foreign trade was ended. Protection of Yugoslavia's infant industries was thereafter no longer available. Woodward does not regard the reform as so important as the declining world prices for Yugoslavia's primary products (such as timber and minerals) that followed. She appears to be misinformed about the share of these in Yugoslavia's total exports: by 1970 they were less than 40%, by 1985 only 20%. All this abandonment of central authority, however, left only international finance and the armed forces under federal control. Even there, central monetary controls and foreign exchange controls were limited, and each republic controlled its own territorial defence forces (TDFs).

Economically, there were very great differences going back over three centuries between the relatively developed North (Slovenia and Croatia) and the less developed South. Most of the industry there was lay in the north, primary production in the south. It had been the aim of the new Yugoslavia of 1945, in the interest of unity, to correct these differences through an element in the Federal budget to support universal social services and through a Fund for the Development of the Less Developed Republics. Economic reforms dictated by the IMF, including the increasing decentralisation of power to the republics, meant cuts in these programmes. As elsewhere under IMF treatment, the poorest suffered worst, so that by 1989, while the average income of the richest republic, Slovenia, had risen to double the national average, that of the poorest region, Kosovo, had fallen to one quarter of the average. That is a 7 to 1 difference. In the 1960s the gap had only been half as wide. (In the UK, by contrast, the gap between Surrey and Ulster is less than 2 to 1.) Unemployment in 1989 had risen in Kosovo to 50% of the labour force, while in Slovenia it was 3.5% and in Croatia 7%. Average rates of unemployment in the southern states including Bosnia were between 20% and 30%, having quadrupled since the 1960s.

What sort of socialist economy could tolerate unemployment?

So much had always been clear to me, but Woodward rightly asks how it could be that a socialist system with central planning controls could generate and tolerate such levels of un-employment, and why the continuing immunity of Slovenia, and to a lesser extent Croatia, from the growing scourge of unemployment? Woodward shows, moreover, that the unemployment statistics reveal only those who presented themselves for work at the local bureaux. She quotes a study made in the late 1960s showing 300,000 officially registered unemployed, plus another 200,000 'on the books' and another 150,000 unregistered, an estimated 250,000 'hidden surplus' among the employed, 1.5 million 'latent unemployed' in agriculture, and 400,000 working abroad. That adds up to a figure of 2.8 million out of a total population of working age of 9 million. Of that total 4 million were independent farmers, so that those who were employed made up less than one half of the rest. In Kosovo and Bosnia it was less than one quarter. (There are some problems with Woodward's statistics which do not always share the same base line.)

Woodward's explanation goes to the root of the dilemma of building socialism in an underdeveloped country. Only Slovenia, and possibly Croatia, could be regarded as falling within the category of developed capitalist economies, where Marx might have expected socialism to be a possible early prospect. First of all she reminds us of the Marxist emphasis on the centrality of the productive process. A clear distinction was drawn by the Yugoslav leaders right from the very beginning between 'productive' and 'non-productive workers', the former being the 'wealth creators', whose increases in productivity with the application of machinery would result in developing economic resources. The latter were needed to provide for health and education and a minimum of administration which should 'wither away' with the steady replacement of capitalist 'management' by the 'free association of labour'.

Woodward provides a useful summary of the Yugoslav rejection of Soviet bureaucratic controls in favour of 'democratic consultation and agreement among autonomous and self-interested but also co-operative property owners (governments and the work collectives with rights to manage social assets) on common rules for value and distribution.' This had clear implications for policy in the Yugoslav leaders' emphasis on what is now termed 'subsidiarity', the 'incentive of individual economic interest operating better', as she summarises it, 'when the decision making and supervision necessary to macro-economic stabilisation were closer to those who actually produced.'

These ideas, Woodward is able to show, long pre-dated the break with the Cominform. Yugoslav 'self-management' was not a response to the disagreement with Stalin, but in part the cause. The exercise of coercive state power, a bureaucratic planning system, forced relocation of labour and collectivisation of agriculture were not introduced immediately after the war as a copy of the Soviet model, but were emergency measures to deal with the crisis in 1948 of separation from the East without being incorporated in the West. As soon as stabilisation was achieved with loans from the United States in 1950, the original aims of decentralised, self-management by 'organisations of associated labour' were reverted to. Election to Workers' Council was begun. The federal administrative powers were reduced, the republics were given back their budgets and their enterprises, and in the phrase of the day, which Woodward quotes, 'the republics' sovereignty was restored.'

But, why did this mean steadily rising unemployment after the late 1960s and especially among women and young people? Woodward's answer is that they were in some strange way 'invisible'. This did not mean that they were to be found mainly among the underemployed in overmanned plants, factories and offices, as in the Soviet Union and Eastern Europe. The requirement of competitive industrial enterprises and of a lean administration precluded that. There were no big lay-offs as under capitalist ownership. The small proportion of the registered unemployed in the total told the true story. At one time nearly one million Yugoslavs in a work force of nine million were finding employment outside the country in Northern Europe. Most of the rest were absorbed into rural underemployment or into the informal economy in the towns.

But why the particularly sharp rise in unemployment at the end of the 1960s? Woodward does not explore the connection between the opening up of the economy to outside competition with the rise in unemployment at this time. The jump in the figures, including those working abroad, was from 10% in 1967 to nearly 20% in 1969. When capitalist economies face such competition wages fall until the labour market is cleared — or that is the theory. The Yugoslav system allowed wages to fall even in the social sector of public enterprises, but this did not lead to more workers being taken on. It does not always under capitalism and for the same reason as in Yugoslavia. Falling profits left no resources for new investment, except in the most advanced enterprises, i.e. in Slovenia and Croatia. This was what disproved Benjamin Wards' thesis. It was not workers' self management but the absolutely low level of development of most of the country that resulted in both falling wages and rising unemployment, when the economy was opened to the world market.

What sort of political economy?

Woodward's first revision in the accepted view of the Yugoslav model was that the model was in the making well before the break with the Cominform. This can be accepted as can her two further revisions of widely held views of the Yugoslav system of political economy. The first is that it was seen as still a command economy, with the commands issued through the Party apparatus and increasingly through that of the Party in the republics. The second is that it was seen as a form of 'market socialism'. In fact, she is able to show that it was neither. There were co-ordinating links between producing units, but these were supplied not by the centre but by the banks and by chambers of commerce, the unions and local governments within territorial units, and there were joint ventures between enterprises in developed and underdeveloped regions.

At the same time, while, as she says, 'markets for final goods operated largely by a free price mechanism and consumer demand which was meant to be the primary incentive to producers', there was no market in 'factors of production — labour, capital and intermediate goods, raw materials, credit in the form of working or venture capital.' This is certainly true, but she goes on:

'Although monetary prices were assigned to facilitate allocation and comparative valuation and a rent was charged on fixed capital and borrowed funds . . . there was', she says, 'no central calculation of shadow prices to imitate a market', such as had once been proposed by the Polish economist, Oscar Lange. But ' price regulation was used in place of a production plan to achieve balanced development as well as monetary equilibrium by influencing incentives to producers'.

I don't think that Woodward is right here. It depends on which period she is talking about. In the 1950s and early 60s there was certainly no talk about shadow prices. But, after the Prague spring in 1968, Ota Šik, the Czech economist responsible for economic planning under Dubcek, fled to Belgrade. He had developed a system of shadow prices in Czechoslovakia and he certainly attempted to do the same for Yugoslavia, by which to show not an imitation of the market, but the value of the stored-up machinery in the value added by production workers. In this way, the incomes' policies introduced by Yugoslav leaders to control inflationary pressures and to provide a basis for fair wage differentials could be made more acceptable to those who were well placed to demand and to keep higher wages and enterprise profits.

Šik does not seem to have had his model of shadow prices formally introduced, but Prime Minister Kardelj at the 1971 congress of self-managers advocated that 'for the same socially acknowledged work (i.e Marx's 'socially necessary labour-time') approximately the same living standards should be secured for the workers'. Trade unions were increasingly 'expected to help co-ordinate the different interests which come to the surface in the sharing of income and personal remuneration.' The basis of this sharing was said to be 'the pooled production potential in the form of living and *past* labour (emphasis added) and their part in the joint financial risk.' Kardelj spoke of 'the clear insight' that workers could be given into the value of their work at different levels of technology, which would lead them to understand the needs of those at lower levels and of investment in new development.

This query about Woodward's understanding of the evolution of Kardelj's thinking in the 1960s and early 70s is part of a wider question I have about her analysis. She appears to have concentrated on two periods — the 1950s and the 1980s — the beginning and the end of the Yugoslav experiment. The middle years are dealt with more cursorily. But these were the years in which major advances were made in the standard of living of the people — and most especially in their educational opportunities and health services. Woodward is less than generous in her appreciation of the enormous changes that were made in the condition of the people in these years. The evidence she provides from the 1980s of the 'overproduction of intellectuals' and of the desperate search of highly educated young people, even in science and technology, for jobs appropriate to their training is a kind of negative proof.

Woodward's period of studies at the Zagreb Institute of Economics in the early 1980s must have shown her how far Yugoslavia had moved from the Third World country it was in the 1940s. I have to add that I myself revisited different parts of the country — mostly where I had been working in the 1940s during the last year of the war and first years of peace, in Bosnia and Herzegovina, and also in Belgrade and on the coast. I went almost every other year during the 1960s and 70s and early 80s, and I have to say that the transformation was total. I wish I could say the same about the parts of Africa or of Russia that I have visited over the same period. There had always been a cultured elite in the main cities of Yugoslavia, but what one found everywhere was a vast new generation of young people wanting and able to discuss every kind of question — philosophical, political, economic, scientific and cultural. It was still a single-party state, which in the end proved to be disastrous for the resolution of the country's problems, but there was nothing (except nationalist propaganda) that could not be discussed openly and written about in books and in the press.

One other consequence of Woodward's neglect of the years between the 1950s and the 1980s is the scant attention she gives to Tito's leadership of the non-aligned movement in the world and of its perceived economic as well as political importance for Yugoslavia. She recognises the value of the trade agreements following the Bandoeng meeting in 1955, which provided oil and strategic materials on favourable terms in exchange for products of new Yugoslav industries such as rayon (although she complains that the switch to oil was to cause problems for the coal mining industry and a large part of the future burden of foreign debt). She also recognises Tito's aim in working together with Third World countries to challenge the unequal distribution of world incomes. But this was not simply pursued to increase the flow of aid to Yugoslavia — in fact non-alignment policies often led to the refusal of US aid. What Woodward calls Yugoslavia's 'Faustian bargain' of Western aid for an independent socialism was in fact not Tito's choice, but forced upon him by the collapse of his non-aligned partners. One by one — Nehru in India, Sukarno in Indonesia, Nkrumah in Ghana, Goulart in Brazil, Ben Bella in Algeria, Kassim in Iraq, Nasser in Egypt — either died or fell from power, often as a result of CIA intervention.

Woodward's models of 'Slovenia' and 'Foča'
It was in the middle 1960s that the most thought was given by Yugoslavia's leaders to the conflicts involved in promoting both equality and development. The real problem to be understood in Yugoslavia, as Woodward sees very clearly, was not the differentials inside the employed sector, but those between the employed and the unemployed, or insecurely employed, and particularly between the situation in Slovenia and Croatia on the one hand and the southern republics on the other. There was an unrealistic assumption that the south would 'catch up' economically. The gap between standards of living in the North and the South, however, came to be reproduced in each region with the exception of Slovenia as a gap between those having secure employment in what was called the social sector and the rest in the private sector.

There had always been a gap between the privileged and the underprivileged in the special position of Party membership. After the early days of 'protection' for 'old fighters' with the partisans, Party membership was largely meritocratic. Already at school, teachers sorted out the 10% who would be received into the Party. Although Djilas, Tito's closest wartime associate, challenged 'The New Class' in a famous dissident book, Rankovic's proposal for a *nomenklatura* like that in the Soviet Union was not accepted and the special shops, so typical of Eastern Europe, had disappeared by 1950. In 1953, the name of the Party was changed to the League of Communists of Yugoslavia to emphasise its federal character and also its regulative rather than directive status. In the end, the Party became, as Woodward quotes a frequent comment from outside its membership, 'a sort of managers' club'. To this division was then extended a far wider gap between stakeholders in the productive and commercial enterprises and in the public services — the so-called 'social sector' — and an ever increasing underclass outside.

Woodward's central thesis is that the model for the whole of Yugoslavia's development was based on the position of Slovenia, the most advanced republic which the others could and should emulate. It is not for nothing that for three decades the leading economics ministers in the federal government — Kardelj and Kidrich — were Slovenes, one of them becoming Prime Minister.

'The Slovene model of Kardelj and Kidric', as Woodward explains it, 'envisioned the state as a body of rule-making experts that needed no authority with independent producers than that afforded by expertise and professional competence.'

'[In Slovenia] the model underlying governmental policies — an industrially advanced, lean socialist core of skilled workers and commercially attuned manufacturers participating fully in Western trade, a settled labour reserve of private farmers and artisans, and a government of experts and local militia — seemed to be the cause of full employment.'

'It was easy to conclude . . . that unemployment in other republics, rising as one went east and south, was due to political interference with that model or to 'cultural' differences.'

'But Slovenia was also the one republic where the initial developmental

and labour supply conditions and existing plant on which the original
Slovene model was based actually held.'

The fact is, however, that Slovenia was not only different
economically but politically. Slovenia was different from the rest
of the country in that the war-time resistance and subsequent
government was much more nearly a true 'popular front' drawn
from all but the most right-wing parties than was possible
elsewhere. Slovenes wanted a federation as a defence against
outside powers, but insisted from the start on their political
autonomy and economic self-sufficiency. Their need for the
protection of a federal state did not, however, extend to
supporting protection for Yugoslav producers whose costs were
above those outside. Slovene (and Croat) industries were
competitive in outside markets, so long as they were not
encumbered by high cost local supplies. After the collapse of
non-alignment, markets for primary products from the South
were largely in Eastern Europe, where trade was carried on
through bilateral agreements, which did not require competitive
prices. The antagonism was built in from the start. Slovenia
needed the loans to the federation that came from the West for
its development and could pay for them. Slovene enterprises
could also pay for imported industrial inputs. The rest of the
country increasingly could not.

As soon as foreign trade was liberalised — after 1964 —
Slovene enterprises set out to import many materials from outside
and to attract foreign investment. Nearly all of this went to
Slovenia or Croatia. The federation as a whole for long relied
on its Third World-type primary product exports. Woodward
exaggerates the length of time this lasted, but she is wholly right
about the bad effect on the Yugoslav South's economic
development of guaranteed Russian and East European markets
for Yugoslav products whatever their cost, and of the loss to the
South of its markets in the North of the country. The conflict

between the demands of Slovenia and Croatia and the capacities of the rest of the country led to the continual stop-go of Yugoslav external borrowing and finally to the accumulation of unsupportable foreign debts.

Outside of Slovenia and Croatia, apart from different political and religious histories, there were two essential economic differences at the founding of the new state. In the South, where over two-thirds of the population lived, there was practically no industrial plant to start from and a large underemployed surplus labour force on the land. Industrialisation was never able to take up labour as fast as it was released from the land. Slovenia actually imported labour. Labour in Croatia as well as Slovenia had special opportunities, from geographical proximity and cultural tradition, for migrant employment in Northern Europe as well as service employment in the Adriatic tourist trade.

Woodward calls the working of the Yugoslav system outside of Slovenia and Croatia the 'Foča model'. This is for two reasons. Foča was one of the poorest districts of Bosnia-Herzegovina — with a mixed Moslem and Serb population — on the edge of the mountains of Montenegro, where the Partisans found refuge after being driven out of Serbia by German and Axis forces in late 1941, and where some of their fiercest battles took place in 1943. Foc'a was also where, in 1942, Mose Pijade, the Partisans' idealogue, elaborated what came to be called the 'Foča Regulations'.

In an area of food shortage overwhelmed by a liberating army and thousands of families which had provided Ustashe (Axis) soldiers, where the need to win support was essential, looting was a capital offence. Everything had to be shared. Woodward might have added that army soup kitchens provided free food even for 3,000 members of Ustashe families before the harvest in 1942. But more had somehow to be produced — more food, housing, clothing, boots, tools, arms. The land of absentee owners and of proven collaborators was confiscated after court martial, but property rights were not challenged, richer peasants being required to supply tools and take in refugees. Markets were not controlled, but prices were kept down by release of stocks where profiteering was discovered. The army worked with the grain of local co-operative traditions and through local elected committees, but everywhere took the initiative to establish new productive capacities. There were workshops and mini-factories as well as hospitals and schools wherever the Partisans could find concealment in the woods and mountains.

From this war-time experience and from the facts of an overwhelmingly agrarian society outside the north and west of the country, Woodward draws her concept of the developmental 'Foča' approach, which had to be concerned with creating the very conditions for economic growth. This was quite different from Slovenia, where the concerns of the 'liberals' were with 'mechanisms and institutions for the "rational" allocation of resources that were largely given.' The 'Foc'a' lands of the South had, like other regions of the Third World, to be developed on the basis of their natural resources — agricultural products, water power, forests, rocks and mineral reserves. Their development took the form of purely quantitative increases, based on the application of labour, steady and disciplined work, in large-scale enterprises, with workplace supplies of goods as the incentive to increased production. At first, there were certainly elements of coercion as the South of the country became 'one great construction site' and this was more pronounced after the break with the Cominform. The logic of this development required state protection of local supplies, often produced at high cost, against outside suppliers, whereas the Slovene model depended on competitiveness in outside markets.

The decentralisation which Slovenia and Croatia asked for became the model for the whole country. After the victory of the 'liberal reformers' in 1964, Woodward records that developmental economists were purged in Belgrade. Every republic set out to have its own advanced industries just like Slovenia and Croatia — a steel works, oil refinery, chemical works, paper mill, sugar factories etc. — and then its own engineering and light manufacturing. This had been given early encouragement from the centre by the decision, in 1949, following the break with the Cominform to concentrate defence industries in Bosnia, furthest from the borders, even moving some plants from Slovenia and relocating 100,000 workers. But the 1960s saw a shift in policy. The army and air force wanted the more advanced equipment available from outside or from Slovenia. The policy was established of obtaining one-third of military supplies from the West, one-third from the East, and one-third from inside the country. Bosnia suffered serious deindustrialisation in the 1980s, resulting in large increases in unemployment.

Comparative advantage

The southern republics from the mid-1970s onwards began to go through the same experience of other less developed countries. Their economies had a comparative advantage only in primary products. The price of these in world markets steadily fell year by year in relation to manufactured goods. World-wide primary producers sought to make up for falling receipts by producing more, encouraged by the IMF and World Bank to repay their debts from export earnings. But this only pushed prices down still further as stocks built up. In Yugoslavia more money was borrowed to step up industrialisation, to escape from dependence on primary production. But the result was not a great success.

Because of Yugoslavia's political structure each of the southern republics wanted to have its own complete range of industries, whatever its comparative advantages. National liberation had meant liberation from economic as well as political dependence and 'what Slovenia can do we can do'. Global market integration favoured light industrial production. World prices not only for primary products but also for the output of heavy industry were falling. Increasingly, however, a huge surplus capacity was built up and the Southern factories being the least competitive and having no protection against foreign products sought protection within the limits of their own republics. This they often won, but it did not get them protection from outside. More and more they lost out on funding from federal investment. Slovene and Croatian enterprises complained at development funds being wasted in the developing regions and had their contributions reduced. The southern regions were also penalised because building new plant was always more expensive than modernising existing plant.

The result was the steady rise in unemployment in the South and even in Serbia which stood geographically and economically between the North and the South. As Woodward emphasises, unemployment had always been assumed to be absorbed by return to the land or withdrawal into the informal (often black) economy as everywhere in the Third World. Lay-offs were for many years never wholesale, in their thousands in large industrial concentrations, as they are under capitalist ownership. Sackings were of small numbers at a time and spread over a wide area. By the 1980s this was no longer true. The unemployed could not be absorbed and movement between republics was restricted. Yugoslavia had ceased to be a single market. This was a total denial of all comparative economic advantage. Only a third of national output and a fifth of capital movements had come to circulate between the republics, the rest moved inside each republic or in the case of the northern republics between them and the outside world.

Yugoslavia had not only ceased to be a national market, it could no longer be managed from the centre. Unemployment had become uncontrollable in the South where demographic pressures of a rapidly growing population were strongest. The Party, which had for long been little more than an elite club, had disintegrated into its republican parts. Yet the central authority of a nation-state integrated into the world market was responsible for repayment of foreign debt to Western creditors. Debt payments began to absorb 30% of all foreign earnings. More and more production had to be exported — primary products from the South and increasingly manufactured goods from the North. As world prices of primary products declined, the South felt cheated and as the North's manufactured exports left the shops empty, prices began to rise. Inflation at 15% in the 1970s rose to 40% in 1981-3, thence to an average 200% in 1985-8 and finally to 1300% in 1989. The dinar became valueless.

The failure of reform

The conclusion which I had drawn from the impact of inflation on Yugoslavia's divided population was that many people in the North would be exempt because they would have access to *deutschmarks*, which became the only acceptable currency when the local currency, the *dinar*, was being daily devalued. Their *deutschmarks* would have been earned either by work in Germany as *gastarbeiter*, or from the tourist trade, or from work in companies with joint German or other foreign ownership. The rest would be driven to slave for those with real money or to steal and, in the last resort, to kill. This seemed to me to be adequate explanation for the killings, taken together with the total breakdown in social order which large scale unemployment, especially of the young people, brings with it. Slovenia and Croatia, once they established their independence, could issue their own money and give it strength with assistance from abroad. I now recognise that Woodward's emphasis on the traumatic results of 'socialist unemployment', unemployment even in the social sector, is even more telling.

The fact is, moreover, that the last Yugoslav prime minister, Ante Marković, succeeded in 1990 in stabilising the *dinar*. Inflation was brought down and the trade balance improved. But this was short-lived. He failed for three reasons. First, he had done nothing to build up support for his Party, the Alliance of Reformist Forces, for the federal elections due at the end of 1990. Many of those who might have supported him were in fact suffering from his economic measures, which were cutting public spending without any corresponding social policy. The very cuts in federal budgets were forcing people to look more than ever to the republics. Second, Slovenia and Croatia held elections which were little more than referendums on national sovereignty. When the radical nationalists won, the Serb nationalists too saw their chance. No federal elections were thereafter possible, and the newly legitimised leaders of Slovenia and Croatia looked at once for outside support for their moves towards independence. In March of 1991 the European Parliament declared that

> 'the constituent republics and autonomous provinces must have the right freely to determine their own future in a peaceful and democratic manner and on the basis of recognised national and internal borders.'

Thirdly and most importantly, Marković's appeal to Western creditors and to the European Community for financial assistance was rejected, only the Italians supporting this. In other words, the federal reform solution to Yugoslavia's crisis was never given a chance. The United States no longer saw Yugoslavia as a key support against the Soviet Union, since the whole Soviet structure was dissolving. The Europeans followed the leadership of a German chancellor who needed, in order to stay in power, to win Roman Catholic votes in Bavaria by a policy of friendship with the two Catholic peoples of Yugoslavia and a demonstration of historic German interest in the Balkans.

The link between Susan Woodward's two books is the combination of a deformed industrialisation in Yugoslavia, perpetuating the North-South divide, the North accounting for less than one-third of the country's total population, and a special form of protection everywhere for those in the privileged social sector of employment, itself accounting again for less than a third of the total work force. Kardelj's cosy picture, as Woodward describes it,

'of stable socialist communities combining the productive incentives and distributive solidarity of industrial wage earners and small property owners (the alliance of workers, peasants and free professionals) applied to an ever diminishing number of people . . . There was instead a growing urban underclass of unskilled workers and rural migrants; an ever larger stratum of managerial and professionally trained people seeking public sector, non-industrialised employment, and deindustrialisation in poorer regions.'

The leaders of the two Northern republics believed that they could immunise themselves from the contagious spread of the disease. As soon as there seemed to be no longer any military or economic advantage for them to be had through staying inside the federation, they sought to leave it. The advantage had ceased when the collapse of the Soviet Union deprived Yugoslavia of special treatment for US aid. At the same time, outside of Slovenia and Croatia, the steady erosion of the protection of the privileged social sector left even the beneficiaries of the system dispossessed. When the Marković government, in 1989, ended the property rights of the workers in the social system, they who had been the privileged found themselves out in the open with all the private employees, the unemployed whose ranks were swollen by returning migrants from a Northern Europe in recession, all joining the underemployed on the land or the gangs in the cities. They looked inevitably for protection and found it in their national identity, but in conflict and no longer in brotherhood with those of other communities.

Woodward's sombre conclusion to her first book was written as the fighting began but before the full horrors of the war in Bosnia had occurred:

'the historical memory of antagonisms among its separate nations was at best a tertiary factor . . . In the war over land and local community that resulted, it was predictable that the latent conflict of the underlying division of socialist Yugoslavia — between the public and private sectors of employment — would explode into class war.'

Woodward does not pursue this class analysis in her second book, except as one element in the wars to create new states and to emphasise the openness to recruitment into nationalist forces of an 'underclass', particularly in the towns where there were concentrations of unemployed and casual workers in the grey and black economy. I do not accept that the wars in Yugoslavia were class wars, except here and there where Muslims perceived themselves as an underclass. The concept of class implies some kind of recognised horizontal unity, but the Yugoslav system had never permitted this to emerge, not even within each of the republics. Without the protection they had long enjoyed, particularly in the civil service and the army but also in failing industrial collectives, those who found themselves dismissed or demobilised sought for identity in their national origins alongside the already dispossessed. Nowhere was this more evident than in Bosnia with its different communities, where the nationalist leaders on all sides sought desperately to appeal over class divisions. They had to, to survive. And they needed also international recognition of their political jurisdiction and claim to resources.

How outside intervention raised the nationalist stakes
The central theme of Susan Woodward's *Balkan Tragedy* is that outside intervention based on a false or confused understanding of the underlying problems in what had once been Yugoslavia again and again encouraged the very violence of the nationalist forces it was designed to alleviate. The collapse of a system of political protection through employment, given that horizontal class and political associations had been precluded, resulted in the emergence of desperate attempts by individuals and families to find national community protection. But, the power of nationalist leaders to grant such protection depended, as the old federation broke up, on the recognition and support they received from outside the country.

In the elections of 1990 in Slovenia and Croatia, the nationalists (led by ex-Communists) did not in fact win a majority, only the largest number of votes of any Party. But international support for the federal government of Ante Marković was slipping away throughout 1990, and the EC statement of March 1991 confirmed EC acceptance of Yugoslavia's dissolution. Nationalists in Serbia followed enthusiastically where Slovenes and Croats had led — it was, as Woodward insists, that way round. The first victim was the army, which after the break-up of the Party was the one remaining force representing Yugoslavia. But, as Woodward argues,

'In treating its presence in Slovenia and then in Croatia as an illegitimate aggressor, the EC transformed the Yugoslav Peoples' Army (YPA) into an independent actor in the political contest, moving, with each forced retreat from territory declared sovereign, from trying to hold Yugoslavia together and protect army assets to devising and defending a state-building project of its own.'

The United States ambassador in Belgrade had already warned the federal government publicly, in February 1991, during the army's troop movements in Croatia, that the US would not accept the use of force to hold Yugoslavia together. As Woodward notes, this was just a week after the attack on Baghdad. The United States was too heavily engaged in the Gulf War to entertain further involvement in Europe. This did not deter the EC under German leadership from recognising, in December 1991, both Slovenia and Croatia, although an EC mission under Judge Badinter had pointed to the absence of civil rights of Serbs within Croatia's frontiers. The official argument employed was that recognition would deter what was seen as Serb aggression (as Woodward comments 'in their view the cause of the war'). The same argument was used four months later by the United States to persuade its allies to recognise Bosnia-Herzegovina, where an independent republic had been declared in October 1991. It led at once to the establishment at Pale of a Bosnian-Serb government, which had been in formation since June.

What Susan Woodward's careful analysis of events in the break-up of Yugoslavia reveals is that, far from there being clearly established protagonists — the Serbs, the Croats, the Bosnians, the Macedonians — there were nationalist leaders seeking to win control over lands and resources — and over people's minds. Even in Slovenia, Woodward quotes an estimate that a quarter of the workforce was not Slovene, but there were no questions about the territorial boundaries there and unemployment was not a problem until large numbers of refugees arrived, and then the gates were soon closed. In Croatia there were great numbers of Serbs who had lived there for generations. Bosnia, as we have seen, was a multi-national state in almost every one of its parts. Woodward surprisingly refers to it as multi-ethnic. In fact, all its inhabitants were Slavs, but of different nationalities, the Muslims having won the right in 1972 to call themselves a nation. What this meant must engage us in a moment. Here it is necessary only to recognise that, whatever the claims of Izetbegovic, Bosnia-Herzegovina was not in any sense a Moslem state, not even a state with a majority of Moslems in it.

What was happening, as Woodward insists, was that the several nationalist leaders were appealing to national sentiment and the desire of people for protection, in order to claim possession of land and control of resources, and to win international support for their claims. If the Serbian and Croatian leaders had for long been discussing the partition of Bosnia between them, and there is much evidence that they had, this could only be at the expense, even the destruction, of the Moslems. I happened to be in Banja Luka shortly after the German army withdrew in 1945 and was billeted with the Catholic bishop, who had supported the Ustashe and was under house arrest. I was allowed to speak with him and asked what would happen to Bosnia now. He took me to a map on the wall of his study which showed the line drawn in AD 395 north and south through the middle of what is now Bosnia, designed then to divide the Eastern and Western Christian churches. 'We dig a broad ditch along that line and put the Orthodox (Serbs) on the east and the Catholic (Croats) on the west'. 'And the Moslems?,' I asked. I guessed the answer but hardly expected the vicious tone when it came — 'In the ditch!'.

It was above all protection which the nationalists were offering to those who were desperately seeking protection. Much of the fighting in Bosnia, as Woodward demonstrates, took place under the leadership of local commanders, often with para-military support. It was designed very precisely to protect families of one of the national communities against the others. The shelling of cities like Sarajevo was not so much designed to capture Sarajevo as to deny its plurality of communities; and the Moslem nationalists were just as prepared to add to the shelling to win over outside opinion at crucial moments of negotiation, as Woodward is able to show.

On the larger canvas, whatever was thought and suffered locally, such deceptions could help to win sympathy outside to establish support for a larger share of the territorial carve-up on the outsiders' maps, none of which recognised the original plural societies in each district. This is what came to be called 'ethnic cleansing'. It wasn't ethnic and nothing was cleansed, but by so calling it, the outside powers could claim that their intervention was necessary for the defence of innocent people. In reality they had their own agendas — the German government to win Catholic support, the British to get an opt-out from the Maastricht Treaty, signed at the end of 1991, the United States to please Turkey and the other Islamic allies of the USA in Western Asia at the end of the Gulf War.

It is perhaps important to explain here the extraordinary resonance of the word 'protection' as it was used in Yugoslavia.

Proteksia is not even a Serbo-Croatian word, but entered the language perhaps from Italy to mean some special influence among the authorities. You needed it to jump the queue for any kind of benefit. Without it you could wait for ever. You got it through your status as a worker in the social sector or, if you were outside that, through friends or relatives in positions of authority. As we say in England, 'It is not what you know but who you know that counts.' It is a pernicious system, and the tougher the situation and the more unequal the distribution of power the more pernicious it is.

The rights of peoples and of nations

Woodward quotes Paragraph 1. of the 1963 Yugoslav constitution, unchanged in the 1974 version:

> 'The Socialist Federative Republic of Yugoslavia is a federal State of voluntarily united and equal peoples and a socialist democratic community based on the power of the working people and on self-government.'

The key phrase is a 'federal state of . . . equal peoples', not we have to notice 'of republics'. Yet both peoples and republics were recognised because the constitution provided for six republics and two autonomous regions. Six peoples were constituents — Slovenes, Croats, Serbs, Bosnians, Montenegrins, Macedonians; and each had their own republics. Others were minorities — Hungarians and Albanians — and had a measure of autonomy within Serbia. This was Tito's compromise: first to recognise that there were many peoples outside the republic where they had a majority and second to get over the fact that Bosnians were not a 'people'. Only in 1963 did the Moslems gain the right to be called a 'nation' and they did not have a majority in Bosnia and many lived outside. It was difficult to give to the Voyvodina (where the Hungarians live) or to Kosovo (where most of the Albanians live) the full status of a republic, in the first case because many Hungarians had fought with the Axis, and in the second because the field of Kosovo was where the Serbs had made their last stand against the Turks and been defeated in 1389.

There still remained an ambiguity about 'peoples'. Woodward notes that there is only one word in the Serbo-Croatian languages for people and for nation — *narod*. But the origin of the word is 'people', which only became absorbed into 'nation' as the state builders in the Nineteenth Century created nationalism. There always seemed to me to be an ambivalence among Partisans in the reply to their rallying-cry '*Smrt fašismu!* (Death to fascism!) of *Sloboda narodu!* (Freedom to the people!). In the context there was an implication of brotherhood and unity of all the Yugoslav peoples, but in their minds there was first of all a link to their own people. This was perhaps even clearer in a frequent reference to partisans as *najbolji sinovi našega narodu* (the best sons of our people). Woodward quotes this without the 'our' and with people in the plural. There can be no doubt that, while they were brothers in fighting against the occupation armies, they belonged to their own national community. There is an interesting comparison to be made with another more recent national liberation struggle. Nelson Mandela in his autobiography *Long Walk to Freedom* speaks frequently of 'our people'. But this is sometimes the Xhosa, sometimes all black Africans, sometimes only black South Africans.

Woodward offers four concepts of 'nation' as giving a right to a certain territory: first, a historic claim of a people who 'link their common identity to a prior state on [certain] lands; second, a democratic principle that 'all who reside on a territory have the right to choose their state by popular referendum; third, the United Nations (Helsinki) principle that 'all existing, internationally recognised borders are 'inviolable' and define states; fourth, the realist principle which accepts the *fait accompli* of physical control through military force . . . the principle on which most European states were actually founded.' As she rightly points out, use of the principle of national self-determination to create states was convenient at Versailles in 1919 in order to break up the Habsburg and Ottoman empires, but was 'reversing the west European process whereby states created nations, not nations states.'

The question is of the first importance not only because of the legitimation claimed by nationalist leaders after the dissolution of Yugoslavia for their claims to territory, but because of the whole relationship of peoples with a sense of common identity to the nation-states as they are recognised, for example, by the United Nations. Some of these states may be federations, but most have a mix of national communities inside them. The question which Woodward does not address is whether any nation-state can achieve the generally stated aims of freedom and prosperity for its people within what she regards as the necessary desideratum of 'full global integration.' In such an integration power is most unequally distributed between the several states to the point that some have virtually no power, but their boundaries and constitutions prevent their people from uniting with others to challenge the major wielders of power.

It is a great tribute to Tito that he sought in the Non-aligned Movement to develop an alternative global integration to that of the big capitalist powers and their giant companies. That this endeavour failed is a major source of Yugoslavia's tragedy. Some say that having failed he should have turned to a policy of self-reliance, rather than opening the economy to the capitalist world market. This has become a fashionable academic recipe for Third World countries. But it is one thing to make such a proposal in university seminars and at international conferences. It is quite another to set about the task of building up a quite small national economy from the grass roots, without adequate tools or machines or the economies of scale which can reduce costs. The nation-state is no better a framework for complete protectionism than it is for fighting for position in a global market. Without allies small states are lost, but the alliances have to be built from below. Inter-state agreements tend only to advantage the state's leaders.

Nation or class?

'Building socialism in one country' might just have been a possible project in a whole region of the world such as the Soviet Union or China. It was manifestly ridiculous in a backward country of 20 million people. Even more serious, the narrow concentration on national objectives, once the immediate goal of national liberation from an occupying force is achieved, inevitably excludes the interests of those — and they may be a majority — for whom the increase of national power provides no benefits. Much of that national power can so easily be retained by those who exercise the power — at the expense of the rest. Foreign investment in Yugoslavia offers a good example. It is seen by Woodward simply in terms of a necessary access to outside capital. It is not recognised as tying the management and the wider economy to policies that have nothing to do with socialist priorities, such as greater equality, protection of the environment, or meeting social rather than private needs. And of course, Woodward is quite right to show that the exclusive concentration of policy on national wealth creation leads to this conclusion.

There is an interesting parallel to be drawn from Africa. This has been explored by Basil Davidson, who happens to combine an exceptional experience of Yugoslavia's foundation with a life-long study of African history and involvement in African popular struggles. In Africa, as in Yugoslavia, many peoples with languages and traditions in common are spread across several states, the boundaries of which were drawn for the convenience of colonial conquerors and did not in any way correspond to the perceived identity of the peoples. Many Africans have complained that the perpetuation of these boundaries after independence from colonial rule has been a disaster. General

SOCIALISM AND NATIONALISM

Olusegun Obasanjo, one time head of the Nigerian state, felt bound to confess, in 1990, that

> 'The bald fact is that we have squandered almost thirty years with ineffective nation-building efforts. Our policies were far removed from social needs and developmental relevance.'

There is an evident parallel between Yugoslavia and the diverse communities of Nigeria. There is, as Basil Davidson has so perceptively posed the question, always a latent conflict between the 'national' and the 'social' to which Obasanjo was pointing. It is Davidson's central explanation of the disastrous decline of Africa that what he calls the 'armoured shell of the nation-state' has been the Black Man's curse (Basil Davidson, *The Black-Man's Burden: The Curse of the Nation State*). It was the curse of Yugoslavia. It is not just because each nation within the federation preserved its national identity that Yugoslav socialism failed, but because the whole experiment became itself a nationalist project.

The protection and nurturing of the rights and requirements of the people must be the first responsibility of government. Along with the basic needs of food, clean water and shelter, health care and educational opportunity which must be met, there has to be recognition of the right to work in free association with one's fellows and the right to the free exercise of those expressions of community identity — language, customs, cultural activities — which make for the rich diversity of human life. The leaders of the Yugoslavia which emerged in 1945 from the struggle for national liberation sought devotedly to meet those responsibilities. But in trying to free themselves from either the embrace of Soviet power or the control of international capital, they became encased within that iron shell of the nation-state.

As much as the Yugoslav leaders might try to build links with socialist movements outside, through annual conferences at Cavtat on 'socialism in the world' and in a thousand other ways, and as hard as Tito might work to build a non-aligned Third

Force in the world, the whole structure of a world of nation-states militated against them. The huge resources that had to be allocated to defence, the central role of the Yugoslav Peoples' Army, the concentration of power in a single Party for fear of externally instigated subversion, the purge of dissidents after 1948 and the system of *proteksia*, were all responses of a nation-state to external pressures. All the attempts to establish workers' self-management and to make a reality of the claim of the constitution that the state was based upon the 'power of the working people and self-government' came up against that iron shell.

In the final analysis when the logic of the nation-state for all Yugoslavs could no longer be maintained, each separate nation saw no alternative but to follow suit and create for themselves their own armoured shell. The armaments salesmen of the world descended upon them and nationalist leaders appeared everywhere to grab and to hold whatever territory they could and win international recognition for their 'national rights'. Once recognised as 'nations', they could be received into the United Nations and claim the financial support of the IMF and World Bank, whose assistance is available only for states and never for any wider or narrower groupings. The true interests of the people lie, however, in uniting both above and below the shell of the nation-state. The world's peoples have a real need to preserve their own communities within a wider framework of law and economy. But the globalisation, which Susan Woodward hopefully saw Yugoslavia moving towards before 1989, is a globalisation of capital, not a commonwealth of peoples.

IV

Conclusion: The Lessons

One central theme has run through these essays. It is the 'curse of the nation-state', if I may employ that wonderfully perceptive explication of Basil Davidson's. What was once a vision of national liberation has so often become in reality an 'armoured shell', as he calls it. The framework designed for a benign process of social liberation has been adapted by the builders of state power for their own ends as means to hold diverse peoples together. To do this they have sought to fashion a false national consciousness, which has been used to overlay the deep well-springs of community feeling. This has not been all bad. In building a framework for national cohesion the nation-state builders have had to allow for mechanisms of redistribution from rich to poor — although generally as the result of strong pressures from below.

Protecting diversity

The fear that Marxists have often expressed that nationalism is employed to overlay class consciousness is but one aspect of the curse which is wished upon the people by the nation-state. Far worse for socialists has been what Davidson calls the 'iron shell' imposed upon whole populations by the nation-state, which has enabled owners of capital to divide labour into its national segments, while capital operates internationally. Peoples are thus not only forced together in arbitrary associations that overlay their original communities, but they are separated from their fellow workers in other nations, often working for the same companies but kept apart by artificial barriers of race and nationality. No more awful examples can be imagined than the results of nation-state building that have followed the break-up of former Yugoslavia.

To acknowledge the curse of the nation-state is to recognise the blessings of the rich diversity of human life, which the homogenised nation has displaced. The different tongues, the various customs, the great range of folk music and art, what we call the 'ethnic' crafts and designs in costumes, decorations and utensils — far from these being protected by the nation-state, their survival is only to be found in its purest form where the power of the nation-state has been weakest or only short-lived. The search for 'authentic' crafts has now to take their collectors and connoisseurs deep into the mountains and deserts and backwoods as yet unpenetrated by the all-pervading stan-dardisation of the common market of the nation-state. In my last visit to the *baščaršija* in Sarajevo I looked for something in the bazaar to take back to my wife, whom I first met in that once beautiful city. Anything in a stall window which I admired was, they told me inside, not for sale; it was an heirloom. The objects for sale were not only of crude workmanship, it was no longer possible to distinguish which part of Yugoslavia, or even of Bosnia, they came from.

This may seem a strange plea coming from a socialist for the conservation particularly of what is old. It is not, however, just the preservation of popular art but its encouragement and development in every household that should be a socialist priority. The political descendants in Britain of William Morris do not need to be told that. In the horrors of war in Bosnia the symbolic importance of cultural monuments was clearly revealed — in the Serb nationalists' shelling of mosques and in their destruction of the old town hall of Sarajevo which housed the two million historic volumes of the Bosnian national library, in the Croat nationalists' demolition of the Moslem centre of

Mostar, including its famously lovely bridge over the river Neretva, and in a thousand other acts of wanton vandalism on all sides, the warring parties sought to eradicate the cultural treasures of the separate communities.

National and social liberation

National struggles for liberation, whether from autocratic or feudal rulers or from alien empires, all had the aim of ending the oppression of whole peoples and the inequalities of rich and poor. In other words, they aimed at social as well as national liberation. But the nation-state as an instrument for the development of capitalism was, perforce, engaged in a political economy that by its very nature tended to polarise wealth and poverty, even where there were no monsters devouring the body politic through their hold on all productive facilities. Where the people could not be kept under control by force of arms and the secret police, measures of cohesion were required, which involved some redistribution of wealth from the rich to the poor. It was the breakdown of any such equilibrating social process in Yugoslavia that we saw lying at the bottom of the economic and political collapse of the federation.

Socialists would have expected to find in socialist Yugoslavia not just a necessary measure of cohesion, but a full respect for the equality of all citizens within the federation, which is what its constitutions promised. At the beginning, under the post-1946 constitution, as we have seen, there were measures of redistribution put in place to try to achieve this. Their abandonment, partly under IMF pressure to reduce public expenditure and to decentralise state intervention, was a major cause of Yugoslavia's economic and political collapse. But we have had to learn from Susan Woodward's studies that it is not only a capitalist economy but socialism also that can generate inequalities. The inequalities of a command economy managed by a state bureaucracy were clear enough in the Soviet Union and Eastern Europe, although one of the main causes of inequality in capitalist economies, the existence of mass unemployment, was absent. What Susan Woodward has demonstrated is that a much more democratic socialist system nonetheless generated unemployment. This was the result of two deep faults.

The first fault which socialists in particular should recognise is one we have already noted. It lay in the failure to correct the original inequalities in endowment between the North of the country and the South. When economic growth is a chief objective of policy, it is much easier and quicker to achieve such growth from higher starting levels of economic development. This is true whether one considers agriculture, mining or manufacturing. And in Yugoslavia the weakness of the South was much aggravated by the fall in world prices affecting its main comparative advantage in primary production. The second fault arose from a dogmatic Marxist insistence on the primacy of production and of the social sector in the economy, to the extent that unemployment in the secondary and private sectors was disregarded. This weakness in its turn was aggravated by the failure of the Southern republics to absorb the unemployment that was generated by raising productivity in the social sector and the farm sector through expanded service sector employment. In this the Northern republics were successful and soon began to take the view that, if they could do it, why could not the Southern republics follow suit. The answer that they must be incompetent only opened up still further the first fault.

The scale of a federal state

We saw earlier that James Madison, one of the founding fathers of the United States of America, had insisted that a federation must be on a continental scale, to reduce the opportunity for local populist domination. He would have understood exactly how Slovenia and partly also Croatia were behaving within the

CONCLUSION: THE LESSONS

Yugoslav federation. Madison was no socialist, but the lesson for socialists of one or two states in a small federation dominating the rest is quite clear. At the same time, we have seen that there is another argument for larger scale in federations, and that is the power to negotiate with the giant modern transnational corporation, often backed up by one of the major powers. No Yugoslav government had the scale of resources to resist that kind of power, and governments increasingly became the servants of the international financial institutions acting for the foreign banks and others with investments in the country.

Most of the new nation-states of ex-Yugoslavia see themselves joining the European Union, since they know that they are not big enough to stand up to the giant companies and the international institutions. We have already seen the crucial role which the German government played in gaining the recognition of Slovenia and Croatia by the European Union and then by the United Nations. The United States thereafter insisted that Bosnia be recognised. It could simply be concluded that these new nation-states will become the lackeys of the major European powers and that Serbia will be forced into some form of alliance with Russia. It can hardly be denied that the European Union is very largely the creature of the Franco-German accord. But this Union, as an association of powerful existing states, unlike the United States at its formation, is bound to have some regard for the rights of all its members whatever form of federation or confederation is arrived at.

Such a political and economic association of states as will be likely to form the European Union in the future will have to ensure that the need for cohesion is given a high priority. Otherwise, the Union will quickly break up into its component parts and that is not the desire of its leading members any more than of the smaller states. The Union is bound to act, as the nation-state once did, as a forum for popular opinion and a protection for the lives of the peoples that compose it. Socialists

77

will have to be ready to take advantage of this opportunity as they once took advantage of the framework of the nation-state. That will imply a much greater preparedness than most socialists have shown in the recent past to work and act internationally. It will also imply the most imaginative thinking by socialists about the proper balance of local, regional and central government.

The United Nations

Each of the new nation-states from the old Yugoslavia has been admitted to membership of the United Nations and of its associated specialist organisations including the financial institutions. This confirms what has long been clear that the United Nations is not an organisation of nations but of nation-states. Whatever the rhetoric of the opening words of its Charter that 'We the United Nations do solemnly declare . . .' the rest of the document refers only to the representatives of states, whose 'sovereign equality' is recognised and 'nothing in the Charter is to authorise the United Nations to intervene in matters which are essentially within the domestic jurisdiction of any state.'

It was proposed at the time of the UN's founding, but never accepted, that the one and only supreme international body should comprise a directly elected chamber as well as the General Assembly of nation-state representatives. This may be a lost cause particularly today when it is hard enough for UN officials to persuade member states, especially the largest one, to pay their long overdue subscriptions. The United Nations has been criticised for its failure to bring the fighting in Bosnia to an end at an earlier stage. Those who think that this could have been done by a show of military strength should read the warnings of Susan Woodward, reflecting as they do the views of the UN representative in Bosnia, of the likely consequences of any military action that was not linked to a peace agreement, which was what in the end was achieved, however divisive the result.

CONCLUSION: THE LESSONS

Within the limits of its resources the United Nations did seek to maintain and to protect a life-line of supplies to the beleaguered peoples of Bosnia. Once the die had been cast by Germany, followed by European recognition of the break-away states, that is all that the UN could do. With more resources it would have done the job better, but lack of resources was a decision of the great powers, not of the UN organisation. It was not the heavier armour of NATO but the agreement on peace that changed the situation at the end of 1995. There is much criticism of the UN today, but most people realise that it would be a disaster for world peace if the UN were allowed to be downgraded and the great powers were to be given untrammelled right to police the world. This is not to deny that the UN does need reform.

The most serious need for reform in the organisations of the United Nations is in the financial institutions, whose demands on Yugoslavia in relation to its foreign debts we have had cause to criticise. It is enough to recall that the insistence on policies which gave absolute priority to foreign debt repayment cannot be dissociated from the economic and social collapse of Yugoslavia. And we have seen that this was not a solitary case but has to be recognised as the cause of social breakdown, disorder and even war in other heavily indebted countries — mainly in Africa and Latin America — most of them among the poorest in the world. The so-called 'structural adjustment reforms' imposed as a condition of extended borrowing, or of debt rescheduling, have succeeded only in further impoverishing the great number of the poorest people where these programmes have been applied, while enriching a quite small number both in the debtor and creditor countries. Moreover, all attempts by regional groupings in Eastern Europe or in Africa to develop joint or common programmes of action to escape from the debt crisis have been rejected by the financial institutions in the name of the holy sovereignty of the individual nation-states. The World

Bank, moreover, still rejects even those minimal requirements of accountability to countries in receipt of aid which were originally laid down in its constitution. Socialists must draw lessons from the debt-ridden collapse of Yugoslavia for the future conduct of the IMF and World Bank.

The absence of any direct representation of the peoples in the organisations of the United Nations serves also as a reminder to socialists of the urgent necessity of strengthening all those non-governmental organisations which seek to unite the peoples themselves across nation-state boundaries. There are already established a myriad of international activities of the unions of trades and professions, of artists and sports men and sports women, of environmentalists and peace movements, of men and especially of women who are seeking to realise their faith in a better world than that which they have inherited. They must seem very small by the side of the armies of the great powers and the bureaucracies of the giant companies. But in Bosnia the work of the International Red Cross, the supplies from hundreds of voluntary agencies and the communication systems of non-nationalist journalists, like those associated with the group Alternative Information Media (AIM), contributed very greatly to alleviating a quite desperate situation. Reestablishing professional, cultural, political and other social links between non-governmental organisations in the successor states of Yugoslavia and their counterparts outside should be a particular priority for socialists.

It would be a great mistake for socialists to suppose that the Yugoslav socialist experiment should be written off as an inevitable failure. The fact is that it was destroyed from outside. However attractive at first sight the opening up of free markets and multi-Party elections may seem to appear now to East Europeans, the day will come when people will look back to the best aspects of socialist self-management in Yugoslavia with

CONCLUSION: THE LESSONS

respect and consider what lessons that attempt at economic co-operation may still have for future experiments.

In the longer run the present small scale activities of environmental groups, of alternative trade associations, of unions of primary producers and consumers, and of ethical banks and credit unions will come to challenge the giant corporations and banks and the great powers that stand behind them. Yugoslavs will take their part in making that challenge. It should give us all courage to remember that it was not the dinosaurs that inherited the earth but the descendants of the small and unnoticed primates. Such an evolution will not come quickly, but it will come, if, in the telling words of Noam Chomsky, we are to fulfil our human destiny 'as moral agents and not servants of power.'

Other titles in this series

*Is Socialism Inseparable
from Common Ownership?*
by G. A. Cohen

New Directions for Pensions
How to Revitalise National Insurance
by Peter Townsend and Alan Walker

New Labour's Aims and Values
A Study in Ambiguity
by Ken Coates MEP

Democracy versus Capialism
*A response to Will Hutton with
some old questions for New Labour*
Michael Barratt Brown
with Hugo Radice

Forthcoming

Feminism after Post-feminism
by Liz Davies

May Day
Solidarity, Celebration, Struggle
written and illustrated by John Gorman

The Rights of the Unemployed
A Socialist Approach
by Anne Gray